# How to Succeed in the World Today

T0053939

REVISED AND UPDATED EDITION

# HOW TO SUCCEED IN THE WORLD TODAY

## LIFE STORIES OF SUCCESSFUL PEOPLE TO INSPIRE AND MOTIVATE YOU

# DALE CARNEGIE

MEDIA

MEDIA

Published 2022 by Gildan Media LLC
aka G&D Media
www.GandDmedia.com

Front cover design by David Rheinhardt of Pyrographx

Interior design by Meghan Day Healey of Story Horse, LLC

Library of Congress Cataloging-in-Publication Data is available upon request

ISBN: 978-1-7225-0609-4

10   9   8   7   6   5   4   3   2   1

# Contents

# Foreword

Dale Carnegie, best known as the author of *How to Win Friends and Influence People*, improved millions of people's lives. He had the uncanny ability to awaken hidden talents that they may have otherwise never discovered.

This book contains advice on success from Dale Carnegie, taken from his radio broadcasts from the 1930s. Despite its age, you will be amazed to see how helpful this book can be. One word you read may change your whole life, revealing a magic key to the happiness and success that Carnegie brought to many thousands of people.

The success story that is the life of Dale Carnegie might be summed up in one of his golden rules for success: "Arouse in the other person an eager want." By arousing an eager want in everyone he encountered to follow his guidance to achieve happiness and success, Dale Carnegie's name became synonymous with self-help for Americans as they were recovering from the Great Depression. Since then, his work has changed the lives of countless individuals around the world. Today his teachings continue to be the basis for innumerable programs and personal transformations.

Carnegie found at an early age that he was a skilled orator, and he used this skill to launch his career as an inspirational and motivational speaker. Born in 1888 to impoverished farmers in Maryville, Missouri, Carnegie had to rely on his own resources to make his way in the world. Finding that he couldn't win over others with his athletic prowess, he turned to public speaking. Impressed with the moving delivery of popular teachers and entertainers who passed through his community, he joined his school debate team, where he fine-tuned his ability to influence others.

Being of scant financial means, Carnegie lived at home with his parents while he attended the State Teachers College in Warrensburg, Missouri. Stories of his life state that he practiced reciting speeches as he rode on horseback to and from his classes. Upon graduating in 1908, he spent several years as a salesman. When he'd saved up some money, he moved to New York City to pursue acting, but he found that the stage was not suited for him after all.

Carnegie's career as a self-help leader began about four years after he finished college. Drawing on his oratorical skills, he began teaching evening classes in public speaking at the YMCA. His classes were a hit. His students learned not only how to be persuasive speakers, but also how to create a good impression on others and be confident businesspeople. He opened his own Dale Carnegie Institute after only two years of teaching.

Carnegie's first book, *Public Speaking and Influencing Men of Business*, was published in 1913. As his exposure to successful individuals grew, he became increasingly persuaded that professional success was much more a result of good interpersonal skills than of education, experience, or technical ability. His classes and teachings focused on developing effective social skills, particularly in the workplace. To provide a textbook for his students, he began years of research, reading extensively about the lives and activities of business leaders. The book, *How to Win Friends and Influence People*, published in 1936, was a tremendous hit. It's been translated into twenty-nine languages and has sold an estimated 15 million copies.

The reach of Carnegie's teachings expanded after the book's success. The Dale Carnegie Institute grew; during his lifetime, it had programs in 750 cities across the United States and had established programs in fifteen foreign countries. About ten years after publishing *How to Win Friends and Influence People*, Carnegie followed with another popular self-help book, *How to Stop Worrying and Start Living.*

Carnegie died of Hodgkin's disease on November 1, 1955, at the age of sixty-six. Despite an explosion of newer self-help books written over recent decades, *How to Win Friends and Influence People* remains relevant and useful. Since his death, the Dale Carnegie Institute has continued to expand and is currently a highly respected business training firm operating in many countries.

Shortly after the publication of *How to Win Friends and Influence People*, Carnegie began hosting an enormously popular radio show of the same name as his best seller. While his writings have been available ever since they first appeared, the following pages are predominantly drawn from transcripts of this show, and they offer a long-lost source from which to learn his principles.

In addition to providing stories of those from whom he'd borrowed his rules for success, Carnegie's program demonstrated how to apply the rules in your own life. The case studies of people here, who appeared on his program, reflect the spirit and mentality of those times, which in many respects were different from our own. Although much has changed in the decades since, we still all want to lead happy, full, successful lives. The keys to achieving such happiness and success are no different today from what they were decades ago.

To set forth Carnegie's advice in a logical sequence, this book has been divided into three parts. Part 1 advises readers about developing a positive perspective on their lives and who they are. After the foundation of a positive outlook has been laid, part 2 advises readers how to strengthen good qualities, such as self-understanding and self-confidence. Part 3 sets forth the wisdom for which Carnegie was renowned: how to have fruitful and rewarding interactions with others.

May this compilation be as helpful to you today as Carnegie's words were to his listeners many years ago.

# PART ONE

## *Think Positively about Yourself*

Absolutely everyone, regardless of his or her circumstances, can have a happy, successful life. Everyone can enjoy waking up in the morning knowing that they will experience a joyful, uplifting day. This may sound like nonsense, but it's true.

First and foremost, at the center of our relationship with others is our relationship with ourselves. As simplistic as it may sound, adopting a positive attitude is the essential first step toward our own happiness, and to how we present ourselves to, and are experienced by, everyone we meet.

In the first part of this book, Carnegie shares his insights on thinking positively about ourselves. He knew that our acceptance of who we are and encouragement about who we can become are the foundation upon which we build the lives we want.

# CHAPTER ONE

# Be Positive in Your Thoughts and Actions

The power of positive thinking to dramatically impact our lives is clearly not a new idea: everyone has put it forward, from the writers of the Bible to Shakespeare and on to the present day. It is a fundamental precept of Buddhism: controlling our thought processes is at the core of Buddhist practice. "The mind is everything," said the Buddha. "What you think you become."

We may be inclined to doubt the truth of the power of our minds to shape our lives. We may want to attribute our success or our happiness to circumstances: "I had bad teachers and never learned how to read well!" "My father was abusive, so I only know fear and anger." Our circumstances may be difficult, but how we respond to them is at the heart of our daily experiences and our expectations. If we think, "I have strong comprehension skills, and I can master economics," or "I'm a confident, loving person," we can, in all actuality, begin to experience academic achievement or confidence.

Fear probably defeats more people than any other one handicap in life. A lot of people think they were born with fear. But psychological experiments have proved that a baby is born with fear of only two things: loud noises and the sensation of falling through space. All your other fears you have acquired and developed yourself. So if you developed them yourself, you can get rid of them yourself if you really want to.

Can you? Who is stopping you? Nobody but yourself. Where are these fears of yours? Ever stop to think of that? They exist nowhere except in your own mind. They can't possibly exist anywhere else. And I am going to tell you how to get them out of your mind.

I'm going to give you four suggestions, which you can use to conquer an inferiority complex, destroy fear, and develop courage and self-confidence.

## Four Steps to Self-Confidence

1. Stop thinking of yourself as shy or timid.
2. Act as if it were impossible to fail.
3. Become interested in other people.
4. Do the thing you fear to do.

Do you want to be courageous? All right. *First*, be courageous. Begin right now. Walk out of your house with your chin up, your head in the air, and a song in your heart.

*Second*, act as if it were impossible to fail. One of the most popular books in the 1930s was Dorothea Brande's *Wake Up and Live*, and its main point was: "Act as it were impossible to fail." Remember that the most important thing about you is the thoughts you think. Think thoughts of fear, and you are bound to be fearful. But if you think thoughts of courage and act as if you really had courage, you'll gradually get courage.

*Third*, stop thinking of yourself. Get interested in other people. You are only fearful because you are thinking of what other people are thinking about you and what impression you're making on them. How foolish! Nine times out of ten, the other person isn't thinking about you at all. He is just like you: he is thinking about himself.

*Fourth*, do the thing that you fear to do, and keep on doing it until you get a record of successful experiences behind you. If you are a salesperson, pick out the buyer you most fear to call on. Go and see them tomorrow. When you get in their office, tell them that you have been afraid for years to call on them. If you are nervous and shaky right then, admit it. That will break the ice. Tell them they are so important that the very thought of calling on them makes your knees tremble. They will take that as a compliment. That will make them like you and want to help you.

I am not giving you new ideas. They have been used and tested for thousands of years. If you go out and apply these principles, they will work miracles for you. I know, because I have seen this happen with thousands of people.

All negative thinking, whether generated by fear or resentment or anger, is something that we ourselves create. If we create it, we can certainly create something else in its stead. Yes, it is much easier to give this advice than it is to actually change the negative thoughts that we've grown so accustomed to. But consciously try it out. If you're afraid to ask someone for a date, try telling yourself that you're perfectly comfortable asking that person out, and ask anyway. If you think that you can't jog a mile—"I'm out of shape; it's too hard!"—try telling yourself that you actually can jog that distance, and get to the track.

You'll be amazed at how your positive ideas about yourself will be shared by others. And you'll be delighted to learn just how capable you are, how much you can enjoy yourself, and how completely your experiences and feelings will follow your thoughts.

# CHAPTER TWO

# The Road to Happiness

What do you want more than anything else in the world? That's an easy question to answer. You want happiness. Everybody does.

The answer to being happy, as simplistic as it sounds, is to think happy thoughts. Our experience of every event and every interaction completely relies on how we think about it. Why not think something good?

Novelist Grace Miller White suggests seven ways you and I can be happy. She calls them her seven roads to happiness. Follow these roads, and what a happy person you'll be!

The first road to happiness is: smile! Smiles are contagious. Get in the habit of smiling as soon as you open your eyes in the morning. Smile as you fall asleep at night.

Just listen to what a few smiles did for one young lady. Mary said she was miserable. "How could a person be happy," she asked, "when my mother and sisters are always chewing at each other, seeing which one could bite the deepest? And my young brother! What a pain he is!"

Although Mary was only in her teens, she looked fully twenty-five, because she frowned so much. Grace said to her, "By chance, have you a smile somewhere behind those pretty teeth?" The corners of her lips twitched a little. Mary sighed, and said she never smiled anymore. There was simply nothing to smile about.

So Grace told her she must start making others happy. And to do so she must follow one road: smile!

Grace saw her about a month later. And what a different child! She looked eight years younger. She positively beamed. She said, "Mrs. White, you told me to smile, and I did. And you know, I discovered you can't smile at a person and fight with him at the same time."

It's positively amazing what a flood of sunshine can be let loose by a few little smiles. The American steel magnate Charles M. Schwab once said his smile had been worth a million dollars, and he was probably underestimating the truth.

The second road to happiness is to give for the joy of giving. One woman craved happiness, but when she was asked if she ever thought of making others happy, she said no.

Grace told this woman to keep only one thought in her mind: she must think only of what she could do for others, at least for a week. The idea didn't appeal to the woman very much, but she agreed to try it.

First, the woman practiced on a hungry man. She took him to a restaurant and bought him a hearty meal. Next, she saw a blind boy standing patiently at the curb. She helped him cross the street. That woman experienced a new warmth in her heart. Now those were only little things, but what a miracle they performed! We can all find new happiness with just a few thoughtful acts every day. There is often more real happiness in giving than in receiving.

The third road to happiness is very easy and very effective: look for the good qualities in everyone and everything. After all, if we're only going to look on the bad side of every picture, we can't be very happy, can we?

Rule four is: be happy in spite of adverse circumstances. We can do it, and it's lots of fun. Grace told about a mother who had a dearly beloved son. He was a brilliant boy: an engineer, with several college degrees. Suddenly he was stricken with polio. His mother could have poisoned his life and hers with worries and sadness. But what did she do? Each day she went smilingly on her way, never weeping, never displaying grief. Her heroic fight to be happy was an inspiration. "Conditions could be much worse," she said one day. "My son loves me devotedly. That's all I ask."

If that dear mother could be happy in spite of such misfortunes, surely you and I can be happy in spite of our little troubles. Our happiness depends on our mental attitude. Abe Lincoln used to say, "Most folks are about as happy as they make up their minds to be."

The fifth rule is, fill your mind, your heart, and your hands with love. You'll be surprised to find how it will overcome every hateful thought and experience. People go around criticizing others, yet it's all in their own thinking. If you love with all your might and main, you can't be unhappy about these things.

For example, once a man came to see Grace, and he was so unhappy that he wept. He hated the world and everyone in it. When his sobs had subsided into short little gasps, Grace asked, "Feel better now, don't you?"

"No," he answered. "I'm going to kill myself."

Grace did a funny thing. She helped that man make out a list of the ten best ways to commit suicide. Then she asked him to pick one way—just one—that wouldn't cause anyone any trouble or any pain. "Because you mustn't hurt other people," she said.

For several minutes, the man stared at the paper. Then he asked, ever so softly, "There isn't any nice way, is there?"

"Of course there isn't," Grace replied. "So snap out of it! Live! Now I'll tell you what to do. Get the hate and bitterness out of your heart. Every time a mean or hateful thought comes to you, immediately think of something pleasant, something beautiful. Substitute thoughts of love for thoughts of hate."

In less than a week of this new way of thinking, the man found a nice job with a good salary. "And let me tell you," he said, "when I gave my wife my first paycheck, it was some grand sight."

The sixth rule: mind your own business. To muddle about in someone else's affairs seems much easier than minding our own business, but it can have adverse effects. Grace tells about a very handsome and intelligent man who had an attractive personality and good manners. But he couldn't hold a job.

He said that his employer should have had a sense of gratitude for all he had done.

"A sense of gratitude?" Grace asked. "What have you ever done for him?"

"Oh, I told him where he was wrong, and what's more, I told him about a lot of mistakes he was making. The next day I was fired!"

That isn't surprising. The more Grace talked with him, the more she realized that this fine-looking young man had been interested in the business of everyone but his own. "Mind your own business," she told him. He tried it, and it worked wonders.

Now, for the seventh, and last, rule for the road to happiness: be thankful things are as good as they are. They might be a lot worse. Most of us aren't half as happy as we ought to be, largely because we concentrate on the little, unimportant things that we dislike instead of thinking about the thousands of things for which we ought to be profoundly grateful.

I was walking home from the train one night, and I was a bit unhappy about something; I don't remember what; it wasn't important. I said to myself, "Dale Carnegie, what a fool you are. Think of all the things you have to be grateful for. And here you are, miserable because of some inconsequential thing."

I concentrated for the next ten minutes on what I had to be thankful for, and by the time I got home, I was one of the happiest men in Forest Hills, New York. If you want happiness, keep your mind on the things you have to be thankful for.

These rules work. They take a little effort, perhaps, but reap a rich harvest of happiness.

Our culture and media perpetually tell us that happiness comes from what others say or do ("Every-

## The Seven Roads to Success

1. Smile.
2. Give for the joy of giving.
3. Look for the good qualities in everyone and everything.
4. Be happy in spite of adverse circumstances.
5. Cultivate love.
6. Mind your own business.
7. Be thankful that things are as good as they are.

thing would be OK if only Michael loved me back") or from some external event or thing ("The guys would think I'm cool if I had a motorcycle").

We may think we'll be happy when we get a promotion, but we will find that once we get it, our feelings day in and day out aren't really very different than they were before the new job. What changed was what was outside us, not what was inside. Because our inner conditions are the same as before, our happiness is also the same.

Happiness doesn't depend on outward conditions. It isn't what you have, who you are, where you are, or what you are doing that makes you happy or unhappy; it is what you think about it. "There is nothing either good or bad," said Shakespeare, "but thinking makes it so."

Our happiness depends on our inner conditions. We create our own sense of well-being, our own sense of contentedness, and our own peace of mind. The notion that we find our happiness inside is not new. Eastern religions have long held that we generate our own happiness, and contemporary Western experts agree.

The same is true with unhappiness. If we feel hurt when someone says something unkind, it is because we have decided to respond that way. On the other hand, if we remember that the statement is not so much true as it is a reflection of the person making it, we can walk away without feeling any worse than before.

It is our decision to have loving, happy thoughts, and more importantly, the execution of that decision, that brings us happy lives.

# CHAPTER THREE

# Appreciate What You Have

Relentlessly yearning for things that we don't have is a prescription for unhappiness. This is true no matter what the object of our desire is; it even applies to career success. Being satisfied with who we are and what we have is imperative to having a good outlook on life, and in turn to being a shining presence to those we meet.

Popular psychologist Donald A. Laird wrote a book called *More Zest for Life*. He lays out three things that may kill a person's zest for life.

First of all is too much ambition. I've known a number of people who have suffered from too much ambition. For example, I know of one very famous movie actress. Few women ever drank more deeply of the heady wine of success. She made millions of dollars and won worldwide acclaim. Yet she told me that, in her opinion, extremely ambitious people are seldom happy. Why? Because the more they get, the more they want.

You'd think that this celebrated star would be satisfied with all her outstanding accomplishments. She ought to be the happiest person in the world. But she isn't. The last time I saw her, she told me she wanted to learn French, but she was so busy she didn't have the time to learn French in a calm, unhurried fashion. She had to hire a French instructor to ride with her in her car from one appointment to another. She also said that she loved to take long walks and go horseback riding, but she rarely had time to do either.

Ambition is like food and rest. It's a grand thing, but it can be overdone. If you're too ambitious, you may get to the point where your ambition is driving you rather than leading you.

The whole world is seeking happiness, but it can't always be achieved merely by ambition. I often wonder, for instance, whether gaining the goal of his ambition brought Abraham Lincoln the happiness he expected from life. As a young man, Lincoln broke sod with a wooden plow and a team of oxen. He felt sure that he'd be happy if he could only get ahead in politics. Yet when he reached the White House, he was so crushed by the tragedy of the Civil War that he said he'd been far happier as a barefoot farm laborer back in Illinois than he ever was as president of the United States.

So far, we've been talking only about those who have been fortunate enough to fulfill their ambitions. What about those whose ambitions are never achieved? After all, only about one person in 50,000 can attain a reputation or riches. Naturally, that means that if the other 49,999 happen to crave fame and fortune, they're doomed to disappointment. And falling short of the things you've dreamed of may make you feel inferior. If you don't guard your thoughts carefully, such disappointments may bring you the bitter, long-lasting unhappiness of frustration.

Although we certainly must have some ambition, let's be reasonable. Let's not try to accomplish the impossible. Let's not want too much. Let's not cry for the moon. Let's make our aims in life service to others, a happy family, and a comfortable existence— not wealth or fame or power. As Socrates said 2,500 years ago, "If we can't have what we want, let's want what we have." And 372 years before Christ was born, the Chinese philosopher Mencius said, "To nourish the heart, there is nothing better than to make the desires few."

I'm thoroughly in favor of ambition, but if we don't achieve our ambitions, we shouldn't allow that to spoil our enjoyment of life. And always remember, ambition in itself is not a guarantee of happiness, by any means.

Dr. Laird also points out that many people fail to get the enjoyment out of existence that they deserve because of a guilty conscience. According to a survey made at Syracuse University, one person out of every five has a guilty conscience.

There's no doubt about it: our whole personality can become distorted—almost diseased—through the gnawing of guilt. Many people show poor judgment when they allow a guilty conscience to ruin their lives. Of course, we all make mistakes. But let's profit by them, and then forget them. Ralph Waldo Emerson once wrote to his daughter:

> Finish every day and be done with it. For manners and for wise living it is advice to remember. You have done what you could; some blunders and absurdities no doubt crept in; forget them as soon as you can. To-morrow is a new day; you shall begin it well and serenely, and with too high a spirit to be cumbered with your old nonsense. This day for all that is good and fair. It is too dear, with its hopes and invitations, to waste a moment on the rotten yesterdays.

The third thing that Dr. Laird said could rob our lives of happiness is, to my way of thinking, one of our worst enemies. It's fear! How in the world can a man expect to get any real enjoyment out of life if he's badgered and beset by fear?

As I've already shown, we're not born with fears. They're practically all acquired. But before we're through with life, we find ourselves afraid of all sorts of things. We're afraid of failure, of poverty, of being laughed at, of old age, of change and the new things it may bring, of facts, and of other people. We fear the future and the unknown. We're afraid to stand alone, afraid of losing our job, afraid of accepting responsibility, and so forth. We're intimidated and defeated by fear—miserable, morbid phobias that cheat us of true happiness. We forget that most fears are entirely unnecessary—products of the imagination, false, foolish fears that are merely a result of slipshod thinking. We must face life frankly and courageously. Only in this way can we hope to achieve the true happiness that we all desire.

The first thing a person should do to conquer fear and get more pleasure out of life is acquire self-confidence. Over my decades of conducting courses in public speaking and personality development, I've seen the lives of men and women revolutionized by gaining self-confidence.

If we're going to get anywhere in life, self-confidence is absolutely essential. After all, if we don't believe in ourselves, certainly no one else is going to believe in us. Yet according to some authorities, more than half of all adults are seriously handicapped by lack of self-confidence.

Self-confidence can be developed in several ways. First, practice public speaking; speak before an audience whenever you can. That will do more in a short time to develop self-confidence than anything else I know of. When you lose your fear of crowds, you lose your fear of individuals.

Second, think thoughts of confidence. To be sure, you can't keep thoughts of fear from entering your mind, but you can keep them from staying there. As Dorothea Brande puts it in her book *Wake Up and Live!* "Act as if it were impossible to fail."

Third, get out and do things. Don't sit in a corner and wish you had confidence. You can't develop a strong arm by wishing for one. You can only develop it by using it. The same thing is true of confidence.

Again, if you can't have what we want, want what you have. You might be amazed at how this principle will work to aid your enjoyment of life. Perhaps you have a job that doesn't interest you much. Say you work as a customer service representative for a large food-processing company. Most of your day is spent speaking with people who are complaining about something. You would rather be working in the design department, creating packaging and mar-

keting materials, but at this point, you are not qual-
ified for that position. You could be frustrated and
do your job in a perfunctory way, or you could show
your boss (and more importantly, yourself!) that you
will not let this circumstance chip away at your good
nature.

As you sit down at your desk in the morning, know
that you will provide the most pleasant, comprehen-
sive customer service that you possibly can. Right now,
you will want what you have and stand in excellence
exactly where you are. Everyone you speak with will
hear the graciousness in your voice, and your supervisor will be hard-pressed to avoid recommending
you to others when the right opportunity arises. You
leave work feeling good about what you did that day, a
happy person.

Want a different result? Focus on what you don't
have. In fact, you can keep focusing on it, because it's
much less likely that you will ever get it.

Try another scenario. Let's say that you want to be
married. Once you have a spouse, you will be so happily in love, nothing will ever feel wrong again. You'll
have someone to look after, someone to take care of
you and who will always know exactly what to do to
make you happy. While you are single, life is dull and
empty, and there is nothing to give it any meaning.
You're miserable.

You can see where this is going. Who wants to get to know someone who's miserable? How will you find someone to love and marry if you're so wretched? It is not always easy, but find a way to want what you have. You then get to be the person now that you want to be in the future.

Another tip for developing more zest for life: learn to laugh. A big, hearty ha-ha! No polite chuckling, mind you, but what is known in the theatrical world as a belly laugh. That can be the best thing in the world for you.

Dr. Laird quotes one physician as saying, "Those who laugh the most are the ones that live the longest and enjoy the best health." And Dr. Laird himself says, "What a medicine laughter is! All it needs to make it really appealing is a Latin name and a fancy price, and a label that calls for shaking the stomach well while using."

There's no doubt about it: laughter relaxes us mentally and physically. After all, we can't laugh and worry at the same time, can we? So if you haven't laughed for a long time, you'd better start with a good laugh at yourself. No doubt about it: laughter adds real zest to life.

# CHAPTER FOUR

# Picture Yourself as the Person You Want to Be

As you've seen, I'm an advocate of practicing control over our thoughts. I encourage you not only to think positively but to visualize yourself as a successful, happy person. You can actually make true the thoughts that you have about yourself.

One woman who turned her life around simply by thinking differently about herself was the sister of one of my best friends, and her name was Mrs. Marshall.

Mrs. Marshall had been an invalid for years. She had a leaky heart valve. Her physician warned her that any sudden strain or fright might kill her instantly.

One day Mrs. Marshall walked into the Independence Avenue Bank in Kansas City, Missouri, and presented a thousand dollar bond for payment. The cashier counted a pile of bills and shoved them toward her. Then, with the suddenness of an explosion, things began to happen. Before she could reach for the money, robbers rushed into the bank. Waving their guns, they made the tellers throw up their hands. They threatened to shoot the customers unless they flung themselves face downward on the floor. Everyone obeyed. Everyone except Mrs. Marshall, the erstwhile invalid.

So she was one of those stubborn ones, was she? Well, these gangsters swore they would show her a thing or two. They grabbed her by the arm. They cursed her. They beat her across the breast with a sawed-off shotgun. They threatened to blow her to smithereens. And what happened? Did she die of heart failure? Did she show signs of fear? Did she lie down like all the other customers? She did not. She looked the robbers straight in the eyes and said triumphantly, "God is my protection. I will not lie down. I'll not harm you. Go right ahead with your work, but I will not lie down."

The gunmen were stunned. They'd never seen anything like that before, so they backed away. They robbed the bank, but they didn't take the thousand dollars in cash that lay on the counter in front of Mrs. Marshall. And they didn't make her lie down.

From that moment on, Mrs. Marshall was a changed woman. Where she had previously been a timid, retiring individual, leading a secluded existence, she was suddenly transformed into a woman of abundant energy, with a wide variety of interests and a normal, fearless outlook on life.

What performed this seeming miracle? I know, because, as I've said, her brother is one of my best friends, and both he and his sister have told me the story and explained the mystery. Her body hadn't changed. She had the same teeth, the same hair, the same blood, and the same bones. The only thing that had changed about her was her thoughts. For years she had been thinking of herself as a shy, timid, sickly person, and, as Solomon said a thousand years before Christ was born, "As a man thinketh in his heart, so is he."

Naturally, she was precisely the kind of woman she thought she was. Can any of us think thoughts of fear and be courageous? How can we think thoughts that make us shy and then expect self-confidence? If you tell me what thoughts you think, I'll tell you what you are. That's easy, for your thoughts make you what you are.

Do you want to change your life? I can tell you precisely how. You can do it by changing your thoughts.

I spent an afternoon with actress Mary Pickford during the time she was preparing to get a divorce from Douglas Fairbanks. Many people imagined that she was unhappy. But I found her to one of the most radiant and serene people I had ever met. Her secret?

She's told it in a little book of hers entitled *Why Not Try God?* Here are a few words from that book:

> Whatever is happening to you or to me at this very minute is absolutely the result of what each of us has been putting into our minds, what each of us has been thinking for years. And do you realize that what happens tomorrow will be the result, to a great degree, of what you are thinking today? You and I cannot possibly escape the result of our thoughts.
>
> I haven't solved all my problems yet. But I shall, for I have learned that as I take care of my thinking, my thinking takes care of me in every detail of my life.

Now here is a little bit of philosophy that I took out of my scrapbook from author Elbert Hubbard. Let me read it to you:

> Whenever you go out of doors, draw the chin in, carry the crown of the head high and fill the lungs to the utmost, drink in the sunshine, greet your friends with a smile and put soul into every hand-clasp. Do not fear being misunderstood, and do not waste a minute thinking of your enemies. Try to fix firmly in your mind what you would like to do, and

then, without veering of direction, you will move straight to the goal. Picture in your mind the able, earnest, useful person you desire to be, and the thought you hold is hourly transforming you into that particular individual. Thought is supreme. To think rightly is answered. All things come through desire and every sincere prayer is answered. We become like that on which our hearts are fixed. Carry your chin in and the crown of your head high. We are gods in the chrysalis.

If you operated a factory that was supposed to manufacture ice cream and you suddenly found that it was manufacturing carbolic acid, what would you do? You'd fire your employees, and you'd insist on running that factory in a way to make it produce the products you wanted.

Now the most important thing about any of us is the thought factory that we're operating inside ourselves right now. Is it producing shyness when you want poise? Is it producing fear when you want courage? Then ask yourself this question, one of the most momentous questions you will ever put to yourself: "What am I going to do about it?" Don't ask what your mother or Uncle Bill or sister Mary is going to do about it. They can't do anything to help you. But you can. You and you alone can change your thoughts. So why not begin right now by saying to yourself, "I am going to think courage, and I am going to be courage. Other people have done it. I can do it, and I will do it."

Let me ask you a question that will show you how valuable this advice is. Do you know the easiest way to get out of bed or a morning? Years ago, I discovered that it isn't hard to get out of bed. But it is hard merely to *start* getting out. It isn't hard to be courageous either. It is merely hard to *start* being courageous. So walk up to the next friend you meet, and greet him with enthusiasm. Concentrate all your energy on being the kind of a confident, poised person you desire to be.

As the story of Mrs. Marshall demonstrates, we actually are what we think about ourselves. We can use this fact to great advantage in our program of self-improvement. Look again at the quote from Elbert Hubbard: "Picture in your mind the able, earnest, useful person you desire to be, and the thought you hold is hourly transforming you into that particular individual."

Visualize yourself as the person you desire to be. Such visualization works. A well-known study of basketball players at the University of Chicago offers a great example. The action involved in this thirty-day study was shooting free throws, and each participating athlete had his rate of free throw success tested and recorded before the study began. The athletes were divided into three groups. Members of the first group did not practice shooting free throws, nor did they visualize shooting free throws, and their success rate did not change. Members of the second group, who practiced physically shooting free throws for an hour daily, collectively improved their success rate by 24 percent. The members of the third group, who visualized themselves shooting and making free throws but who did not physically practice shooting at all, collectively improved their success rate by 23 percent. These athletes became the successful players that they desired to be just by picturing themselves as such.

Of course, this is not to say that we don't need to act to fulfill our goals and make changes in our lives. It does mean, however, that by holding firmly in our minds the idea of our best selves, we take on those best selves in truth. Remember too that we alone can do this for ourselves. We are who we think we are: why not think ourselves as magnificent?

# PART TWO

## *Develop Winning Qualities*

Once we've gotten into the habit of thinking positively about ourselves, we can put those thoughts into action. Dale Carnegie was a genius at explaining how we can conduct ourselves in a way that aligns with a good outlook: having confidence and determination and taking good care of ourselves.

The second part of this book provides Carnegie's wisdom on demonstrating the attributes that we desire to have. That will lead to success with others.

# CHAPTER FIVE

# Learn to Understand Yourself

At some point, most people face the question of choosing a vocation. No doubt about it: it's a mighty important problem. Don't forget, you spend a third of your life on the job. If you don't like it or you don't earn enough money, it's hard to get a kick out of life.

According to some figures I saw recently, more than half of the working people in the United States are dissatisfied with their jobs. That's tragic! For as Elbert Hubbard used to say, "If you don't find happiness in your work, you will never find it anywhere."

How can you choose the right job? A prominent educator, Dr. Layton S. Hawkins, has some advice about choosing a suitable occupation. One way is to go to a school vocational counselor. Many schools have them now. They'll help you get a picture of your aptitudes, abilities, interests, and personal traits. They do that by giving you psychological tests.

In addition, you can do three things: First, analyze yourself. Second, find out all you can about the various occupations. Third, fit the two together like a jigsaw puzzle.

To analyze yourself, simply check three things. First, your physical makeup. How's your health? Is your eyesight good? Your hearing, your endurance, your nerves? See your family doctor if you like.

Then you've got to know how smart you are. How do you stand in school? Ask your teachers what they think of your mind. They'll tell you if you have a superior mind, although school marks are not always the best indication of mental ability.

The next thing to do is check up on your personality, your temperament, and your interests. What kind of a person are you? What do you like to do? What are your hobbies? What activities do or did you like in school? Which did you dislike? The same is true with your duties at home. You've done a lot of different things, and you either liked or disliked them. Make a list of them. It's an excellent guide.

Not long ago, a young man decided he'd be an engineer. He liked working with machinery, but when he looked into the profession, he found that engineers rarely operate machinery. Instead, they make the plans and calculations, keep records of performance, and direct others, who do the manual operations. This young man listed his likes and dislikes. He discovered that he had always disliked making careful plans and directing others to carry them out. He didn't like mathematics, didn't like to keep records, and he didn't like analyzing results. So he wisely gave up the idea of being an engineer and ended up by becoming a good skilled mechanic.

Finally, study the different occupations. And let me tell you one thing right now: the idea that here is one and only job that you were made for has been exploded. There are probably a dozen jobs you could handle equally well. So pick the one that suits you best. Then give it all you've got.

You can also go to your nearest public library and ask for an occupational index, which lists the books and articles about the different occupations. Take a look at that index, and then read a book about the occupations you're interested in. Your librarian will also tell you what books to read on how to choose a vocation. Read only the very latest ones. Trends change so rapidly, and a book on vocational guidance may be out-of-date before the ink is dry.

You can find out the duties of a job, the mental and physical requirements, and the training it demands. Is the field overcrowded? What are the opportunities for advancement? How much money can you earn?

A few hours of serious thought may save you a lifetime of regret. Your entire future—your whole life, your happiness, your income—is going to be influenced by the kind of work you choose, so why go at it blindly? Why take such an appalling gamble? Why not go to a vocational counselor for help? At least read some books on the subject. You have only one life to live, and for heaven's sake, plan it intelligently!

To recap, the first step is to simply learn about ourselves. Do we enjoy learning about new scientific discoveries? Or are we more likely to turn to the news about politics, or fashion? Do we like to solve problems, or do we prefer to execute the ideas of others? All of these things tell us something about how we will most successfully and happily develop in our career. We can find all sorts of free career and personality assessment tests. All areas of interest or skills are valuable; we need not think that only certain areas or interests are worth pursuing.

Second, we must take the time to do some research about careers that we think we might like. As Dr. Hawkins suggests, find out about the day-to-day activities of people engaged in those careers, what skills they most rely on, and how they went about working in their field.

If you're living in a time when jobs are scarce, you may need to compromise a bit: take less pay than you'd like, or start in a position that requires less skill than the job you'd like to have. These situations needn't deter you. As we've already seen, we can be happy regardless of our circumstances. We will find that if we hold our current situation in a positive light and do our best no matter what, we'll enjoy each day.

# CHAPTER SIX

# Be Willing to Work toward Your Own Improvement

If we want to develop desirable qualities, we must be willing to put effort into our own improvement. This may sound like a lesson in discipline, and it is! But it's well worth the effort. It's designed to further our success in life—both in our careers and in our happiness as individuals. We are the direct beneficiaries of our efforts to develop an unwavering personal ethic and a pleasing personal demeanor.

## How to Improve Yourself

1. Take inventory of yourself.
2. Start yourself off with enthusiasm.
3. Grasp every opportunity to practice your new resolutions.

4. Don't make excuses.

5. Make definite commitments.

6. Play some games.

7. Do things for other people.

8. Be interested in your work.

Here are eight specific rules for developing good practices and a good personality:

**1. Take inventory of yourself.** As discussed in the previous chapter, take stock of your strengths and weaknesses. Look yourself over calmly and honestly. This is not a time to be overly gentle with yourself, and there's no need to gloss over things about yourself that you might not want to admit. This stocktaking isn't for public consumption: it's for you to use in developing your best self. (If you've been following the advice from the first part of this book—to think positive, happy thoughts—you won't allow a reminder of your lesser qualities to get you down.) That said, it's often advisable to ask the candid opinion of a friend whose advice you value. Find out which habits you should try to acquire and which ones you should get rid of.

**2. Start yourself off with all your enthusiasm at your command.** Early in life, Benjamin Franklin drew up a list of thirteen virtues he wanted to cultivate.

He concentrated on one virtue each week until he had covered all thirteen. Then he went back to the beginning and began again. He kept repeating the process until he had mastered all thirteen virtues. Franklin realized that habit is nothing but repetition. Make the formation of your new habits seem like the most important achievement in the world to you.

**3. Grasp every opportunity for practicing your new resolutions.** For example, if you have decided that you do not smile enough (and as we've seen, smiling actually makes the smiler happier!), start in right now. Smile at yourself in the mirror as you wash your face in the morning, and smile at everybody you meet during the day. If somebody steps on your feet in the elevator or shoves you in the subway, smile at him or her too. If you do this and keep it up, it won't be long before you'll be known as one of the most congenial people in town.

**4. Don't make excuses for yourself.** The great American philosopher and psychologist William James said, "Every lapse is like the letting fall of a ball of string, which one is carefully winding up; a single slip undoes more than a great many turns will wind again." Novelist Edna Ferber told me that she forced herself to work at least six hours writing every day. There were many days, she confessed, when she had nothing to write about, and she longed to do other things. But she kept faith with herself. If you want to form a new habit, don't permit yourself to fail in the application of that habit. Should you stray, immediately return to your program. You need not berate yourself, but don't listen to your excuses either.

**5. Make definite commitments.** Any truly successful athlete is someone who makes definitive commitments. Young athletes, from figure skaters to boxers, practice every day, all year round, in addition to attending to their academic requirements. They don't let the desire for leisure activities affect their devotion to becoming the best in their field. If you decide to do something difficult, keep your goal front and center in your mind and in your actions every single day. Reinforce your commitment by making it public. Tell all your friends about it, so that if you fail to follow through, they will hold you accountable. This will ensure that you retain your devotion to your resolution to the end.

**6. Play some games.** At least once a week, play games that require physical exertion and other games that revolve around a matching of wits, such as bridge or chess. If you engage in competitive contacts (either physical or mental) simply for fun, you can further your sense of good sportsmanship. Such games can help you to develop unselfish habits. They will teach you to obey the rules of good social behavior, add to the charm of your personality, and win many friends.

**7. Do something for other people.** Teach a Sunday school class or collect food for the hungry in your neighborhood. Solicit funds for the Red Cross or another charitable organization. Become active in the Boy Scouts or Girl Scouts. The main thing is to go out and do something for other people. We may think that if we are to achieve anything, we need to focus on ourselves and our own advancement. Although that's true, it is even more effective to think about others. Think about a time when you were really happy. Were you thinking about yourself?

**8. Be interested in your work.** Learn to do your work especially well and put your heart and soul into it. Focusing on the excellence of your work will keep you from thinking about yourself. As your selflessness grows, you will find that others are increasingly attracted to you, and your success will grow as well.

It is widely held that three weeks of repeated effort will create a habit. If, for example, you want to start building your upper-body strength, you might resolve to do push-ups every day for three weeks (preferably at the same time of day). As you do the same thing over and over, the behavior becomes "worn into" your brain. When a behavior is repeated enough times, the brain's synaptic pathways associated with that behavior get accustomed to being used. Thus it becomes easier for the impulses that move across those pathways to do so, and the behavior feels comfortable and natural. Before you know it, you have a habit.

The ideas discussed in the last two rules will be elaborated on elsewhere in this book. The key idea to take away is that you must fully devote yourself to your plan for a new you. Only your own steps can take you along your path to self-improvement. But don't be daunted. Remember, you create what is true about you, and what is true is that you are determined and consistent.

# CHAPTER SEVEN

# Keep Fit in Mind and Body

We know how beneficial it is to get regular exercise. If you work out, you know how good it feels to get up and move, and how much more energized and alert you feel on a day when you've exercised. Furthermore, keeping fit is part of developing the good qualities that will help us live happy lives. We can't help but feel more vital and enthusiastic when feeling healthy. This shows in our demeanor, making us more attractive to others.

Getting the most energy out of your body is one of the most vital problems you face. You need to focus on how you can keep from being tired, and how you can get more done with less effort.

In his book *More Power to You*, Walter B. Pitkin says:

No matter what you do, you tap your energies best by short, frequent periods of rest. These allow prompt recovery from muscular contraction and from the tiny tensions that occur in mental fatigue. The length of the rest periods should vary with the type of work, but long intervals are extremely inefficient. Industrial workers doing "light heavy" muscular work for eight hours a day prove this general law. They accomplish as much in a single day of short, frequent rest intervals, totaling about one and a half hours, as in fourteen days of long, infrequent rest!

In short, a man doing "light heavy" muscular work can accomplish as much in one day by taking short rests totaling one and a half hours as he can in two weeks without taking off any time for rest except sleep at night.

It sounds absurd, so I asked Dr. Pitkin whether it could really be true, and he said, "Yes, of course." He took his facts from George H. Shepard's study "The Effect of Rest Periods on Production."

How can you apply this insight? Relax whenever possible. The elder John D. Rockefeller had a couch in his office, and, busy as he was building the greatest fortune in the world, he knocked off for a half hour every day at noon and took a nap. That probably was the secret of his long life.

Napoleon also had the ability to fall asleep practically at will and frequently took naps for only ten or fifteen minutes at a time. As for Thomas Edison, people used to say that he slept for only four hours a night. That was true as far as it went, but the truth is that Edison took catnaps during the day: he knocked off work, lay down, and went to sleep. When he got up, he tackled his problems with renewed vitality and vigor.

I have been doing that for years. I try to get two naps every day: a short one at noon and a longer one about five o'clock. Since I conduct public speaking courses for adults, I usually work day and night. I find that if I take a nap about five o'clock, I can work right up to midnight with ease and enthusiasm. But if I fail to get a nap at five, I get tired and exhausted. That nap in the late afternoon performs miracles for me.

You may ask how people who aren't their own bosses can knock off and take a nap. Fortunately, it isn't necessary to sleep or even to lie down. You can relax just by using a different set of muscles. For example, if you sit at a desk all day, get up once an hour, stretch, stroll around the office, and look out the window. I recently gave orders in my office for everyone to get up and walk around for five minutes every hour. And I said, "This isn't just permission to leave your desks. This is an order." As a matter of fact, Walter

Pitkin says that this is a much better way to relax than lying down, because when you lie down, you are apt to lose your stride, grow listless, and ruin the rest of the day for work. But by stretching and moving around, you send the blood zooming through a different set of muscles, and you renew your energy.

This is reasonable. In fact, it's so reasonable that the United States Army has adopted this method. Field regulations for the infantry require that the men march forty-five minutes, then halt, adjust their packs, and rest fifteen minutes. After they get warmed up, they march fifty minutes and rest for ten.

People suffering from nervous breakdowns or some sort of nervous disorder occupy half of all the hospital beds in America, according to those great surgeons, the Mayo brothers. We rush through the day at a pace that was never dreamed of before, and if we do not conserve the quota of energy that nature gave us, we will be burned-out shells long before our time.

Here are some rules given by Dr. Pitkin in *More Power to You*:

**1. Relax at least once an hour.** If you stand at your work, sit down, stretch out your legs and relax. If you sit at your work, get up, stretch, and walk around. The whole idea is to remove the strain from the part of your body that you have been using.

You might also try a five-minute meditation break. You can meditate anywhere. Just sit up straight, let your eyes close, and focus on your breath. Make a point of thinking about nothing but the experience of your breath entering and leaving your body. You may not be tremendously successful at this endeavor in a busy office or factory, but it's worth doing even if your mind drifts.

**2. Get enough sleep.** Sleep is the greatest medicine in the world. Find out how much sleep you need, and see that you get it. Go to bed at a regular hour every night. Sleep is a matter of habit, and you can train yourself to fall asleep at a certain hour. Remember that your body has to renew itself every twenty-four hours, so don't start worrying and fretting when you hit the pillow.

Many of us today do not get an adequate amount of rest at night. We may feel well enough to function the following day, but feeling well enough isn't much of an existence, is it? Lack of sleep diminishes our cognitive abilities and makes learning harder. It also can put us at risk for heart disease, heart attack, high blood pressure, stroke, and diabetes. Recent studies show that people who are sleep-deprived are more likely to overeat, contributing to the weight problems so many of us have. It does not benefit us to get more done on a particular day or to have more time to study by depriving ourselves of sleep.

**3. Eat properly.** Different kinds of work require different kinds of food. A man who does manual labor needs heavy, nourishing food: meat and potatoes. But mental workers should be careful not to overeat. There is enough food value in a single salted peanut to see a man through two hours of intellectual work. My own lunch, for example, consists of an apple and a piece of cheese, or an apple and a glass of milk, and I find that sees me very nicely through an afternoon's work.

**4. Watch your weight.** This is almost like rule three. Don't let yourself become too fat or too thin. When you're either underweight or overweight, you're working under a handicap.

**5. Watch your teeth.** I suppose this sounds silly, but thousands of people who are otherwise intelligent are working on two cylinders because they are neglecting their teeth. The same thing goes for shoes. The United States Army examined 30,000 men and found that four out of five were wearing the wrong kind of shoes. So if your feet hurt at the end of the day, something is wrong.

**6. Organize your work.** Your mental health will remain strong if you don't let yourself be driven crazy by distractions. Office workers, keep your desk clear of all papers except the ones you are working on.

**7. Never work when you're sick.** You wouldn't expect a clock to run when it's out of order, so why should you expect your body to? If you're sick, go to bed, call the doctor, and stay in dry dock till you're well. Remember, there is just so much juice in the battery, and the way to make it last is to use your common sense.

In sum, taking care of bodies and our brains through good rest and nutrition is a critical element of our efforts to develop good qualities. We'll enjoy being ourselves more, and other people will enjoy us more too.

# CHAPTER EIGHT

# Be Confident

D o you think of yourself as a loner? Are you happiest when you're reading a good book or out in the wilderness on your bike? Or is this idea really your excuse for not getting involved with other people? Most of us have fears that prevent us from doing certain things. Perhaps we're afraid to drive over bridges, so we always take the long way downtown, or we're not comfortable speaking in groups, so we don't join the events committee at our office. What things do you avoid doing because you lack self-confidence?

Fear of failure, rejection, and becoming anxious (fear of fear!) can cause us to greatly limit the experiences we have and can limit our ability to achieve happiness and success. Having enough confidence to simply go ahead and do the thing that is frightening is both a great challenge and its own enormous reward.

I know a man who has what he believes to be the secret of success. He never had much education. He attended high school only three months, and yet in two and a half years he made more than $3 million. In 1915, he was forty-three years old and discouraged; he had a mortgage on his home and was almost $10,000 in debt. But two and a half years later, he reckoned his wealth in millions. He had been in the food business all his life up until 1915. At that time, he couldn't tell brass from copper, yet in the next two years, he built and owned the controlling interest in the largest brass rolling mill in the world. In 1917, he had never been within half a mile of an airplane in his life, yet he was suddenly made vice president and general manager of the Curtis Aeroplane Company, the largest airplane plant in America.

His name is W. A. Morgan. Although he made his money in the economic boom created by the First World War, we must also remember that back in 1917, there were 100 million Americans that didn't make any progress while he was creating a spectacular career for himself.

Mr. Morgan credits a little book called *The Magic Story*. It isn't very long, you can read it in an hour, but it gave him courage. I have seen courage revolutionize the lives of thousands of men, and it certainly revolutionized his. Mr. Morgan believes courage is the most important factor in the battle for success.

"I was asleep for forty years and didn't know it," he says. "I had no more brains when I was making $1 million a year than I had when I was making $25 a week. The only difference was that I had conquered my fears and developed courage and self-confidence.

In that little booklet *The Magic Story*, I read the following words: 'Whatsoever you desire of good is yours. You have but to stretch forth your hand and take it. Have no fear of any sort or shape. Go, therefore, and do that which is within you to do.'

"I believed those words. I read them hundreds of times. I took that little booklet to bed with me and slept with it under my pillow. I lived its teachings, and I found that I could accomplish things that had formerly been impossible as soon as I conquered fear and believed that I could do anything I tried to do."

One incident that helped him took place during the war. He was trying to get an order to manufacture brass for the British Navy. "To get that order," he recalls, "I had to call upon one of the biggest bankers on Wall Street. I was afraid of these big bankers. I felt they were superhuman, that they were bigger and smarter than I was. My knees trembled as I walked into their offices. Then I discovered that one of the most famous financiers in America hadn't read my telegram clearly; he made a mistake in making out my contract. I saw immediately that these so-called big men are just as human as you and I, and just as liable to make mistakes. From that day on, I never feared any man, no matter how big he was."

Mr. Morgan says anyone can accomplish more if they will only believe; then they can act accordingly. "We set limitations on ourselves," he says. "We can't do things largely because we don't think that we can. I used to tell my associates that I would fire them if they ever said a thing was impossible."

It's true that some things are impossible. You can't jump over the moon, for example, no matter how much confidence and courage you have. "But," says Mr. Morgan, "we can get nearer to the moon than we could years ago simply because the Wright brothers in Dayton, Ohio, believed that they could fly and had the courage and confidence to try to fly when everyone laughed at them. Faith will remove mountains. I know, because I have seen faith perform miracles right in my own life."

I believe that fear defeats more men than any other one thing in the world, and I know we conquer fear by willpower, by thinking thoughts of courage.

Fear doesn't exist anywhere except in the mind. But even if fear is only an idea, it can be utterly defeating. Many leaders have recognized the power of fear to dispirit a people and lead to their demise. Napoleon held that there are four elements that go to make an army: size, training, equipment, and morale. He said that morale was more important than the other three put together. In other words, an army's confidence, courage, and willpower had more to do with its success than its size, its training, and the number of its guns. Confidence and courage are just as important in the battles of business as they are in the battles of bullets.

How can you develop courage? Exercise it. Just as you would develop a strong arm or a strong body by exercise, so must you develop your courage by using it. Ralph Waldo Emerson advised, "Do the thing you fear to do, and the death of fear is absolutely certain."

If you know someone you are afraid to call on, call on that person tomorrow. You may be so scared that you have to walk up and down in front of his home or office. As I've already pointed out, this will not make the other person laugh at you. He will feel that he must be very important in your eyes, or you wouldn't be afraid of him. Moreover, he'll understand your experience: there's no doubt that he has been afraid of someone during the course of his life, and he'll respect your courage in facing him.

Increasing our self-confidence could be stated as a simple two-step process. First, we must think thoughts of courage. If we tell ourselves that we're doomed to failure, that will be true. You don't hear politicians tell the media that they think they're going to lose an election. They think thoughts of confidence, and they express those thoughts. This not only establishes the "fact" that they are successful in their own minds, but it sends the message to everyone around them that yes, they are successful. Others hear that message and might vote for that politician. They would not want to vote for someone who has told them that he is going to lose. Why bother?

The second step, even if we haven't mastered the first, is to do the frightening thing. Feel the fear, and do it anyway. When you get to the bridge, keep driving straight. Show up at the committee meeting and offer to help out. Once you've done the thing (or things) that put you ill at ease, you'll become increasingly self-confident, realizing that in fact you can do it. As your confidence grows, you may not even notice that the fear quietly gets smaller and smaller. The time comes when you no longer have the fear.

# CHAPTER NINE

# Develop Your Determination

A positive quality that we'll want to cultivate in our self-improvement program is determination. We might view determination as one part willfulness and one part balance. Willfulness, unchecked, may often do us more harm than good. We've all experienced someone willfully maintaining a position in the face of clear facts to the contrary. This person appears to be unreasonable and stubborn; he or she is not someone we want to socialize with or have on our team at the workplace. But with balance—a willingness to take a stand that is objective and to doggedly work toward a positive outcome—willfulness becomes an asset. This determination will lead us to achieve all sorts of goals, make us desirable companions and coworkers, and bring us great personal satisfaction.

A positive attitude is central to success and happiness, but we can't rely solely on our thoughts to manifest good in our lives. We need to have determination to attain what we want.

As W. A. Morgan's story indicates, thousands of men have reached their pinnacle of success after forty. In one study, medical authority W. A. N. Dorland found that four hundred of the world's most famous men were, on the average, fifty years old when they produced their greatest works. And most of them were producing with superb results for many years after fifty.

For instance, when he was seventy-four, Giuseppe Verdi gave the world one of his masterpieces, the opera *Otello.* After he was seventy, Commodore Cornelius Vanderbilt increased 120 miles of railroad to 10,000 miles—and added the healthy little sum of $100 million to his fortune. At eighty-three, William Gladstone began his fourth term as prime minister of England. At eighty-three, Alfred, Lord Tennyson gave us his sublimely beautiful poem "Crossing the Bar." At seventy-three, William Wordsworth was given the greatest honor that can be bestowed upon an English man of letters: he was made poet laureate. And at seventy-nine, George Frederic Handel gave to the world his beautiful *Triumph of Time and Truth.*

Washed up after forty? Ridiculous! Look in *Who's Who.* Nearly all of the famous people in it—98 percent, to be exact—are over forty. And what do you suppose is the average age of the officers of the biggest industrial, commercial, and financial organizations in the United States? Fifty-eight!

I spent an evening in the dressing room of the late Howard Thurston, the king of magicians, the last time he appeared on Broadway. He told me that he never reached the height of his fame until he passed forty. Actor Lionel Barrymore told me the same thing.

So why sit around twiddling your thumbs and wishing you were ten years younger? You can start in to learn a new trade or anything on earth you desire to learn up to forty-five at least, and perhaps later, says one of our most noted psychologists, and you can start to learn at forty-five with the most comforting confidence of complete success insofar as your age is a factor.

Why not take advantage of your assets, your poise, your knowledge, your experience, your ability to do better work? Why not do as countless resourceful men and women have done? A career for you after forty? Certainly! It can be done! Time and time again it has been done.

Famed New York restaurateur Alice Foote Mac-Dougall told me, "The last thing in the world I expected to do was earn my own living. When I was a little girl, I had everything my heart desired. My family was wealthy, and I was brought up to be quite as useless as the other young ladies of my day. If anyone could have been less equipped to go into business, I'd like to know her.

"At twenty-one, I married a gentleman who was apparently well-to-do. But three months later, I was badly disillusioned. And ten years later, the crisis came. My health was broken. I was penniless. All I had in the world was three little children. And somehow somewhere, I had to earn enough money to feed my babies.

"I sewed. I sang. I made preserves. I did anything to bring in a few pennies. I scraped along this way for several years until I finally realized that I simply couldn't support my growing children with these odd jobs. There was only one thing for me to do: I had to go into business for myself. I was forty years old at the time, and I looked at least fifty.

"I broke my way into the coffee business. That was my husband's business. He had made a most delicious blend for our own use. So I decided to set up a mail-order business and sell this same blend of coffee. I only had $38 to my name, but I rented a tiny office on Front Street in lower Manhattan.

"I managed to sell a little, but we were horribly poor. There were bills and more bills, and nothing to pay them with. I used to arise at six o'clock in the morning and come home late each night. And will I ever forget those cold winter nights, when I went around delivering coffee from door to door?

"Yes, sometimes I'd get pretty discouraged and feel that nothing could ever turn out right, that I'd never again be happy. But at times like that I'd rally myself by repeating over and over those famous lines from poet Browning: 'One who never turned his back, but marched breast forward, never doubted clouds would break.'

"Life challenged me. My devotion to my children challenged me. I simply could not say, 'Fail,' even when things utterly beyond my control affected me.

"One time, just as I was getting established, the market crashed. Another time I was forced to move. This meant new letterheads—added expenses—at a time when every penny had to count. And once a delivery strike paralyzed my business. I often wondered how in the world it would all end.

"I was spending about $2,000 a year in advertising my mail-order business," Mrs. MacDougall continues. "'Now if I could spend the same amount in a little shop,' I reasoned, 'I would have a personal contact with the public, and I believe I'd get better results.' So I managed to borrow some money, and I rented our little shop in Grand Central Station.

"We only sold coffee then, and even that didn't work out very well. The man who rented the space to me said nearly 300,000 people would pass the door every day. So visions of sales amounting to at least 100,000 pounds of coffee a day arose before me. But how many pounds do you suppose we actually sold the first day?

"Five! Exactly five pounds of coffee! Of course, we did a little better after that, but at the end of two years the auditor said my son and I were taking terrible losses. 'Close your shop,' he said.

"'I can't do it,' I replied. 'Give me just six months more.'

So things went along rather dully, until one windy, rainy day. The corridors of Grand Central were packed with a damp mass of miserable humanity. 'Wouldn't it be nice if I could help some of these poor people?' I thought. So, on an impulse, I had my waffle iron sent from home. I made waffles and coffee, and I served them free. And everyone liked them so much they simply insisted that I serve waffles and coffee every day (not free, of course). At the end of five months, the tide had turned. A waiting line half a block long awarded my persistence.

"That was the beginning of my chain of restaurants. The next restaurant was the Cortile, on Forty-Third Street. At the end of our opening day, I never expected anyone would ever have a chance to eat there. I was never so discouraged in my life! You see, there was a clause in the lease that said no smell of cooking would be allowed. I told the owners that waffles would not smell. And I honestly believed they wouldn't. Imagine how I felt when the air became blue with smoke from the waffle iron! The place fairly reeked with the odor of waffles! Sarah the cook simply went to pieces. So I had to cook as well as serve that day! At night, I was face-to-face with another crisis in my business. All the future growth and profits snuffed out in a cloud of waffle iron smoke!

"But luck was with me! I persuaded the owners of the building to be patient until I could install a ventilating system. And so I kept the Cortile. At the end of five years, I had built six restaurants, and the business was worth $2 million.

"Hardships are good for one. The more one struggles, the more one grows. Cold, hunger, and pain are nothing. They pass."

Mrs. MacDougall certainly found a career after forty. "Anyone can," she says. "It isn't how old you are. It isn't who you are; it isn't how much you know; it's what you do and how much will and imagination you put into what you do. The only way to conquer is to walk in where the battle rages most fiercely, and fight— fight until you win! And you will win, if, deep down in your heart, you're determined to win."

In 1930 Mrs. MacDougall decided to sell her six restaurants and retire. But two years later, the new management failed. "I had the tragic experience of seeing all that I had dreamed and worked for about to be reduced to nothing," she recalls. "There was nothing else for me to do but make a fresh start." Eventually she had four of her restaurants back, all in very prosperous condition.

That, I think, is the most inspiring part of her story. To be able to build up a wonderful business success after forty is really an achievement to be proud of. But how much more faith and persistence it must have taken to see all this fall into ruins and then have the spirit and willpower to build it up all over again.

Mrs. MacDougall has a little motto that she says has worked wonders for her: "It's just three little words: push, perseverance, and prayer." That's really beautiful—and vibrant with common sense too.

William James once said, "What we do compared to what we could do is like comparing the waves on the surface of the sea to the ocean's great depth."

Vash Young was a popular inspirational figure and the author of several successful motivational books. However, his early years were full of struggle and hardship. Mr. Young blamed his early failures upon himself; his own thoughts were his own worst enemy. He suddenly realized that by changing his thoughts, he could change his life. He drew up a list of good qualities he wanted to possess and determined to think these qualities, live these qualities, and be these qualities. The nine qualities he decided would turn failure into success were: love, courage, cheerfulness, activity, compassion, friendliness, generosity, tolerance, and justice. Mr. Young admitted that it was a hard battle to change his life over so completely. But he was determined and he finally succeeded, and at the same time he succeeded as a businessman.

Determination and application are two of the first requisites in any undertaking. If you make up your mind to achieve something and really go after it with hard work and perseverance, you'll find you're getting ahead almost before you know it.

Mrs. MacDougall's motto may be quaint, but it's well worth remembering. All we need is push, the motivation to take a risk and make the effort; perseverance, the willingness to keep at it, even when we seem to be flailing; and prayer, the faith that we will experience the perfect outcome.

# CHAPTER TEN

# Seek Opportunities

Perhaps you're lucky, and you just always seem to be at the right place at the right time. But what if, like the majority of us, you're not? You'll have to make your own luck by seeking out ways to advance your career.

Jason F. Whitney never attended high school or college. In fact, he got all of his formal education from a little red country schoolhouse. Yet he became president of the Kraft-Phenix Cheese Company and later director of the Chicago Civic Opera Company.

I ought to be able to speak about this man with authority and feeling because when I first came to New York from the Middle West, he and I lived in a rooming house together. In fact, for one whole year, we shared the same room and bed.

At one point, Mr. Whitney was working in a grocery store. The doctors warned him that he had tuberculosis. They said that if he didn't give up his job, get out in the sunshine, and get some rest, he would be dead within six months. But he had a wife and family to support, and he couldn't quit. So instead of dying as the doctors prophesied, he became one of the healthiest and most successful men in the country.

Mr. Whitney attributes his success to hard work, but he can't have succeeded solely because he worked hard. My father on a Missouri farm has probably worked harder than Mr. Whitney ever did, but he hasn't made a fortune.

You can't expect to succeed unless you do work hard, but hard work alone isn't enough. I think there are several other factors, and one of them certainly was an undying determination to succeed.

Mr. Whitney got his first job working in a butcher shop. "I worked there for my board and clothes," he recalls. "I didn't get any salary at all. I got my board all right, but I never did get the clothes I was promised, so I quit."

Even at that time, he was determined to be the head of a big business concern.

His next job was delivering milk. "I got a job that gave me my board and paid ten dollars a month," he says. "I crawled out of bed at one in the morning. At two, I was out delivering milk. We didn't have any milk bottles in those days, so I carried the milk can and a measure with me.

"My milk route ran through the poorer sections of a mill town. I remember I used to walk into those shacks at two o'clock in the morning. Sometimes there were so many in the family that half of them would be sleeping on the floor. I'd step over their bodies to get into the kitchen to leave the milk. I delivered milk from two to nine in the morning. From three in the afternoon until seven in the evening, I spent in the country getting more milk for the next day."

Yet he still visualized himself at the top. "I figured there was less competition at the top. In spite of the fact that I didn't have much education, I felt that I could get there and that I would get there. Yet I knew I would never get anywhere delivering milk in a small town. So I headed for Boston, where the opportunities were."

He got a job with the S. S. Pierce Company, which produced groceries. "I took a special interest in the cheese department," he says, "and I used to ask all the traveling salesmen about how their cheese was made. I even read books on cheese and studied it from every angle. Finally, after about seven years, I was made head of the cheese department."

When he was working for S. S. Pierce selling cheese behind the counter, instead of wasting his lunch hour, he used to grab a sandwich and a cup of coffee or a milkshake and go out and try to sell cheese wholesale. "And I used to walk home at night to save a nickel on carfare," he remembers. "So I would make stops on my way home, trying to sell cheese to the merchants along the way."

That's tremendously significant. That showed he had enthusiasm for his job; he wasn't watching the clock or trying to see how little he could get away with. He kept on year after year doing everything in his power to serve the company. People who do that usually get ahead.

Mr. Whitney quit S. S. Pierce because he felt that opportunities there were limited. When vacation time came, he bought a ticket to Canajoharie, New York, where the Beech-Nut Packing Company was located. He saw the president and told him that he had always admired the company's products and wanted to work for him.

Beech-Nut gave him a job traveling in New England, and a few months later they sent him to New York to take care of their cheese department.

Here's another big factor in Mr. Whitney's getting ahead. When he was head of the cheese department for Beech-Nut, he advised them to do away with the department—the department of which he was the head, mind you. He felt that because cheese was a perishable product and the company's other products weren't, they could save themselves a lot of extra trouble and expense by getting rid of the department.

Can you imagine the impression Mr. Whitney made on that company when he told them they ought to do away with his department? How many men would have had such courage and unselfishness?

Beech-Nut did do away with their cheese department, and they made Mr. Whitney manager of the chewing gum department. His job was to put out a chewing gum that had never before been on the market in New York without a penny for advertising.

"I'll admit it was a tough job," says Mr. Whitney. "Nobody had ever heard of Beech-Nut gum. Furthermore, we charged 60 cents a box for our gum while the other manufacturers were only charging 48 or 50 cents. We sent the salesmen around to the wholesalers and jobbers, but they merely laughed at us.

"We put gum in places that had never sold chewing gum—restaurants, butcher shops, barber shops—wherever people gathered. We didn't ask the owner of the shop to pay for the gum. We merely left him a box and said, 'If you can sell this gum, you pay us 60 cents, and you keep 40 cents. If you can't sell it, we'll come and take it back.' Nobody could object to that! We left the gum on consignment. The system worked like a charm."

That involved far more than hard work. It required original ideas along with resourcefulness. Mr. Whitney didn't merely think about selling gum. He thought about how the butcher and the restaurants could increase their income without investing any of their capital whatsoever. In other words, he thought in terms of the other man's problems and how to solve them. In my estimation, that's the kind of thinking you must have to get ahead in business.

In addition, Mr. Whitney did a wonderful job of educating himself. He had hunger, determination, and resourcefulness, and he got things done. Small wonder he got ahead!

I remember the night when I came home and he told me he had resigned from the Beech-Nut Packing Company because the job was too easy. "I began to lose interest in it because it was no longer a challenge," he said. "Things were running too smoothly. I wanted to do something that was difficult to do. I wanted action."

The man who quits a job because it is too easy is not the man who fails. That's the man who is going places.

At that point, Mr. Whitney felt that it would be a good idea to join a comparatively small concern, where he would have a chance to get to the top. So he went with the Phenix Cheese Company. He interviewed with the president and sold him on the idea of becoming his assistant. When the Phenix Cheese Company consolidated with the Kraft Cheese Company in Chicago, he was president of that organization for three years, until it merged with National Dairy Products.

Let's sum up the principles Mr. Whitney used so you can use them to get ahead yourself.

First, he had an undying determination to get ahead. He was determined to be the head of a big company even when he was working in a butcher shop. Now I believe a man must faithfully hold in his mind the picture of himself as the successful man he would like to be. That will make him do the things that are necessary to bring about success. However, he has got to be able to work hard, and he has got to have horse sense. I know a man who always had a picture of himself as being up at the top, but he lacked these qualities. He lacked stick-to-it-iveness. He jumped from one thing to another. He was impractical, a dreamer, and his ambition never got him anywhere. He met with failure and frustration and became embittered.

Second, I think Mr. Whitney succeeded because he put his heart and soul into his work. He had such enthusiasm that he even spent his lunch hour selling cheese. I believe that kind of enthusiasm is more important to business success than superior intelligence.

Third, he was constantly seeking opportunities. He left a small town to work for one of the most outstanding companies in Boston. When he saw that his progress was going to be slow, he switched to Beech-Nut Packing Company. When they didn't give him enough work, he joined the Phenix Cheese Company as assistant to the president. That was a smart move. In other words, he was constantly looking for advancement and doing the things necessary to bring it about.

Fourth, he practiced the quality of stick-to-it-iveness. He started in the cheese business in Boston, and he had such faith in it that he ended as president of the Kraft-Phenix Cheese Company.

No one today will advise you to walk home from work so that you can sell some cheese to your local deli. But they might just advise you to follow Mr. Whitney's example in seeking opportunities. Ensuring our own good by looking for avenues in which we can advance is a quality that we want to have.

Interestingly, Mr. Whitney got ahead by looking out for the interests of others. He made an effort to improve his employers' business during his spare time and even recommended that his own department (and hence his own job) be eliminated as out of step with the rest of his employer's efforts. While thinking about others' needs will be discussed later in connection with developing good relationships, it is also a great skill to employ in your own personal growth.

If we seek opportunities with an eye toward assisting someone else in reaching his or her goals, we're much more likely to achieve our own success and prosperity. This is all the more true if we're working for ourselves: what we provide to our clients and customers, whether it's a new wall in their house or a strategy to improve their products' market share, must be in keeping with their desires if we are to develop a thriving business.

Like Mr. Whitney, we'll want to always look for new ways to serve in order to support our advancement efforts.

# CHAPTER ELEVEN

# Use Your Time Wisely

We get frustrated, even angry, when we feel that our time has been wasted. Oddly, however, the same types of feelings don't arise when we waste our own time. This is remarkable, especially since our own waste of our time is something that we can actually control. Perhaps our lack of indignation with ourselves for twiddling away the hours explains why we're so apt to do so.

On the other hand, how good do we feel when we have spent our time well? Isn't it gratifying when we feel accomplished? Think about how you feel about yourself after doing something you find valuable, whether it's writing a thoughtful letter or listening to your great-aunt's stories of her childhood. (Meaningful ways of spending time often result in our own improvement, but they don't have to.)

Then think about how you feel about yourself after doing something you don't find valuable. Perhaps you drive to the store three times a week just to see what's new, or you find yourself getting caught up in news about some celebrity. Meaningless ways of spending time are subjective, of course, but let's face it: you know by your own barometer when you're killing time.

All of us at some point fail to take full advantage of our time. Opportunities to use time poorly change a good deal over the years, but the opportunities to use it wisely have not changed much at all. It's still important to use your spare moments in bettering yourself, but there is also the need for relaxation and rejuvenation.

Time is something that everybody has, but few of us make the most of it. Years ago, I was in Paris shopping for dinner and trying to buy some produce at the market. The vendor became impatient because I took so much time examining the different vegetables, and he began talking to me at a furious rate. He was speaking French, and I couldn't understand a word until finally he said in English, "Time is money."

That expression is so well known that the French don't even try to translate it. Yes, time is money in every language and every country. Time is life itself. Others may possess more money, power, or fame, but no one has more time than you. And you will never have more time than you have now. How you spend your spare time will largely determine where you will be five years from now.

A few years ago, a man in one of my public speaking classes held up his hand and said, "I don't know how I'll be a success in business. I never finished college." I told him that he didn't need to go back to school: by devoting his leisure time to study, he could, within a few years, have the equivalent of a college education.

The average college student, as you well know, does not spend every waking moment studying and attending classes. The average person who wants to better themselves has nearly as much time for study as the student does. Today, on average, people have many hours left outside of the time that they take for work, sleeping, and eating and that they can devote to their leisure occupations. The trouble is not that people don't have time. The trouble is that they do not do anything useful with it.

Successful individuals will certainly devote some time to relaxation and rejuvenation, but they do not spend time in idle pursuits. We can devote a few hours to study and self-improvement. When you go to bed at night, ask yourself, "Do I feel accomplished?" Chances are, you feel as though the evening just passed you by. But in reality, you passed it fruitlessly.

As a young man many years ago, George East-man, of Eastman Kodak fame, worked all day in an insurance office and then worked most of the night developing his idea for making photographic films. As is often the case, George Eastman didn't have to do this all his life. His business expanded until he became the greatest camera manufacturer in the world. He then had leisure for travel and music and the things that he loved. He looked after his time, and his time looked after him. Eastman's example provides is as valid today as it was in his era.

Your time is without a doubt the most valuable thing you possess. Make it work for you.

If you found twenty-four crisp, new, $100 bills in your hand every morning, what would you do with them? Would you spend a few of them wisely and let the rest flutter out the window? Of course not, but that's precisely what most of us do with something even more precious than money: our twenty-four hours of time each day.

People often say that they're too busy. But a lot of people only think they're too busy. They run around in circles. Yet if they invested their time instead of wasting it—if they really did a little intelligent planning—they'd be astounded at how many more pleasures and accomplishments they could squeeze out of one short day.

I interviewed the late Dr. S. Parkes Cadman, the well-known clergyman and writer, shortly before his death. When I think of what he accomplished in one day, I feel like a loafer. He got up at seven o'clock; dictated twenty or thirty letters; wrote 1,500 words for his newspaper column; prepared a sermon or worked on a book he was writing; visited five or six of his parishioners; attended two or three meetings; gave a talk or two; dashed home; read a new book completely through; then called it a day and got into bed at about two o'clock in the morning.

If I had to do that for even one day, I'd be dizzy; but Dr. Cadman kept it up month after month, year after year, until he was over seventy years of age.

How in the world did he do that? I asked him that myself. He said there was no trick at all. He planned his work, and that's the secret of getting things done. Planning your work!

Franklin L. Bettger used to be third baseman for the St. Louis Cardinals, but he injured his arm years ago and had to give up baseball. So he took a job collecting installments for a furniture store in Philadelphia. That lasted for a couple of years. Then he drifted into selling life insurance. At the end of the first year, Frank Bettger was a total failure, and yet five years later, he became one of the leading insurance men in America.

He said his first job was to discover why he couldn't get ahead like other men he knew. He gave that question a lot of thought until it finally dawned on him that he lacked courage, confidence, and the ability to speak well. So he took a course in public speaking.

It worked wonders. Still, other men in his organization were doing ten times as much business. He figured that it wasn't because they were ten times better salesmen, but because they were ten times better organized. So he began to budget his time. He planned his entire twenty-four hours. Certain hours he allowed for study of his business, such as reading good books and newspapers; others for recreation. He set aside certain evenings for the theater—and for time to think. He spent one hour every Saturday completely alone and devoted this hour to hard, concentrated thinking.

"I honestly believe," he said, "that one of the chief reasons why most people fail to get ahead is that they don't plan their time. I'm really convinced that it's just as important to budget your time as it is to budget your money."

When Frank budgeted his time, the first step was, each Sunday he would write up a program for the coming week on a large sheet of paper, which he kept in a loose-leaf book.

I asked Frank to take me through what he had done the previous Wednesday. He replied, "I got up at seven o'clock. It takes me thirty minutes to shave and take a bath." It may sound as if he doesn't accomplish much in those thirty minutes, but he says, "That's the time of the day when I concentrate. It's the most difficult mental exercise I ever practiced, but it works miracles."

By 7:45, he was dressed and read the paper until breakfast at eight o'clock. At 8:30, he left for work. "Wednesday afternoon is my time for golf, so I quit working at noon. Then when I got home, I planned Thursday's work."

Although he plans his week in advance, he can only plan his actual work at the office from day to day. "So I did that before dinner on Wednesday," he told me. "After dinner I read the *Meditations* of Marcus Aurelius for one hour and spent half an hour thinking about what I had read.

"After that, I listened to the radio, read the paper, and walked. And here's an important point: I always save these moments of recreation until the end of the evening. If I didn't do that, I'd never get around to my hour of serious reading. I make myself do first the things that I would really like to do last."

That certainly shows self-discipline. I asked him, "Frank, don't you find that all this planning makes a rather routine existence?"

"Yes," he replied, "it does make a routine of routine things. But it places routine things in their proper order, so that you're not a slave to routine all your life.

"I not only plan my time in advance, but at the end of each day, I also keep a record of the calls I've made. The minute I fail to do that, I find I don't make as many calls.

"By keeping a record of my calls, I've been able to work out some figures that prove that every call I make—regardless of whether the man is in or not—puts exactly $2.30 in my pocket. So if I feel rather lazy, and I'm thinking, 'I guess I won't bother calling on John Smith today. He's probably out, and he's not interested in buying any insurance, anyway; I'll just skip him!" I remind myself that I'm throwing away $2.30 if I don't make the call. That gives me the incentive I need to get out and do it, for I've discovered that the more calls a man makes, the more sales he makes. It's the old law of averages; you can't beat it.

"I honestly believe self-organization's absolutely essential," added Frank. "Any man or woman who is worried, dissatisfied, and weary of the eternal struggle without much to show for it is undoubtedly poorly organized. It takes time and effort, of course, and you may not make much progress when you first try it. But keep at it, and you'll win.

"And remember this: don't start out with too ambitious a program, because this business of planning your time and sticking to schedule is difficult at first. If you attempt too much, you may get discouraged, so make your first month's program easy until you get the idea. Don't attempt too much, but see it through at all costs. Believe me, it's worth it!"

It was certainly worthwhile for Frank; it helped him become one of the highest-paid insurance men in this country. As a matter of fact, I've tried to put this idea into practice myself. And I've worked out four specific rules that have been particularly helpful to me.

**1. Spend at least one half hour a day just concentrating, on your business problems, for example.** This period of thinking should be at a time when you're doing something else. Frank likes to concentrate while he's dressing and shaving, but I usually listen to the radio at that hour of the morning, so I concentrate when I'm walking to and from the railroad station. But no matter when we take this mental exercise, the important thing is to spend one half hour a day just concentrating.

**2. Spend at least half an hour a day in a reflective mood.** By that I mean, seriously think about yourself. Think about what you're getting out of life, where you're weak, what you can do about it, what you want to do, and why you're not doing it. I do this often. Not as often as I ought to, but my average is fair. In his book *How to Live on Twenty-Four Hours a Day*, author Arnold Bennett suggests walking home from work as an ideal time for this reflection.

Time spent in contemplation or meditation, when we deliberately stop engaging in thought, has been found to be enormously beneficial in diminishing stress and providing the practitioner with a peaceful mind. You can then turn this mind to problems at work or difficulties at home. A peaceful mind is less likely to be put out when its owner is stuck in a long, unproductive meeting and is more likely to address a project's requirements without getting distracted.

**3. Use every spare moment of the day.** Those scattered minutes offer a wonderful chance to improve your mind.

At one point, Dr. Cadman was working as a pony boy down in the coal mines. (In those days, ponies were lowered into mines to haul the coal from one spot to the next, and a pony boy led the ponies around the mine). He always had to wait a minute or two each time his cart was unloaded; and while he waited, he would dive into his pocket and pull out a book. He seldom had more than 120 seconds at a time, but by using them he read himself out of that mine. Similarly, Abraham Lincoln studied law while working as a grocery clerk. I used to buy a book I wanted to read, tear out two pages at a time, stick them in my hip pocket, and read them during my spare time.

Why don't we all make use of our time like that? Think of the hours you spend just riding elevators, to say nothing of the countless minutes we waste each day waiting for the bus or the train. All of these moments could be turned to good use.

**4. Plan your evenings so that you'll have a good balance of study and recreation.** Read good books. Attend evening classes. Spend one night a week on some new subject. For instance, study birds one season, or delve into the amazing secrets of biology, or the fascinating story of mankind. Develop hobbies. Remember, how you spend your time will very largely determine where you'll be five, ten, or twenty-five years from now.

Don't act as if you're going to live forever. That sounds modern enough, doesn't it? Well, Marcus Aurelius, the old Roman emperor who used to write down his thoughts while he was fighting wars and ruling his far-flung empire, first said it about 150 years after the birth of Christ. Marcus Aurelius lived about as busy a life as anybody could live, and yet by using his spare time, he was able to write a work that is now treasured as one of the most precious legacies of antiquity: the *Meditations*, which Frank mentioned.

Don't act as if you're going to live forever! I think we need that advice today as much as the Romans needed it eighteen centuries ago. We plunge headlong through the years without planning our lives, without taking time to live, without pausing to do the things we really want to do. Before we know it, alas, it's all over. Yes, we really do act as if we were going to live forever.

Do you know how long you're going to live? No? The life insurance companies do. They figured it out by studying the life records of millions of people. They don't know how long you as an individual will live, but they do know on an average how long someone of your age will live.

Say you're forty-two. Say your life expectancy is eighty. That leaves thirty-eight years, right? Say you sleep eight hours a day, and you work eight hours a day. You will spend nine years dressing, eating, and doing miscellaneous things. That means you have only nine years left in which to work—only nine years left to achieve what you want to achieve.

I have often felt that we need a new type of doctor—not one who will feel your pulse, take your blood pressure, or tell you to cut out coffee, but a doctor of the fine art of living. A doctor who will sit down with us and say, "Are you doing the things you dreamed years ago you would do? Are you leading the kind of life that you will be satisfied with when you look back at it across the years?"

The chances are that we aren't. It is so easy to get in a rut. It is so easy to drift. It is so easy here in America to devote all of our lives to making money. For example, a student in one of my classes stood up one night and said that for years he had dreamed of nothing and thought of nothing but plumbing supplies. What a confession! Even if I knew he would make a million dollars, he would have only my pity. If the United States Steel Company telephoned me tomorrow and offered to pay me a salary of $1 million a year for the rest of my life with the understanding that I was to devote every hour of my waking time to working for the United States Steel Company, I would say, "No, I am not interested."

I shall not pass this way again, and I am far more interested in making a life than I am in making money. So all of my time is not for sale to anybody, at any price whatever.

I want to make a plea for all of us to devote a part of our lives to reading good books, to developing hobbies, to widening our interests. Let's get out of our ruts. Let's wake up and live.

Charles Darwin is the author of a book that I would rather have written than anything else that has been produced since Shakespeare wrote *Hamlet*, yet Darwin admitted at the end of his career that his life had been too lopsided; he wished he had lived it differently. He said if he had his life to live over again, he would listen to some good music and read some good poetry every day.

Are we too busy to do that? We just think we are. The busiest and most important men in history have found time for good reading. In 1912, when the first convention of Theodore Roosevelt's Bull Moose Party was in session in Chicago, bands were playing underneath Roosevelt's rooms at the Congress Hotel, and thousands of people were surging through the streets yelling, "We want Teddy!" Amidst all the shouting and tumult, Roosevelt sat in a rocking chair in his room, reading the Greek historian Herodotus. Ah, Teddy Roosevelt was a busy American who led a well-balanced life!

When Teddy Roosevelt reached England on his way home from his African hunting expedition, he did not ask for someone to tell him how England solved her political problems. He asked for a guide who was familiar with the songs of the native birds to take him through the English countryside.

Once when he was in the White House, Roosevelt telephoned a well-known Washington correspondent to come to the Executive Mansion at once. This newspaper representative wired his employer and asked him to have the presses ready to dash off an extra containing the important political news that the president was ready to divulge. When he arrived, Roosevelt didn't say a word about politics. Instead, he led the reporter out into the White House yard and, tingling with excitement, proudly showed him a nest of young owls he had discovered in a hollow tree.

Years ago, a friend of mine was visiting a prominent businessman in Detroit. This man turned to my friend and said, "Would you like to meet Henry Ford?" He said, "Yes, of course." So that afternoon they drove over to Ford's factory, and Henry Ford came down and got in the car with them. They started toward an adjoining town to attend a meeting of some kind; I believe it was a hospital board. On the way, they had to pass through a stretch of woods. As they were going along, Ford leaned out of the car and said, "Listen, do you hear that? Stop a minute." The driver thought something had gone wrong with the car. Without saying a word, Ford got out of the car, walked a short distance into the woods, and stood gazing up at a tree. Presently the other two men joined him, and they found that Henry Ford was listening to the song of a bird—a brown thrush. "Isn't it beautiful?" Ford exclaimed. "That's the first one I heard this season." I don't know whether Ford was a better businessman because he was interested in birds, but I'll warrant he was a happier man.

I want to make a plea to you to spend one night a week studying some new subject. Andrew Carnegie made one of the greatest fortunes the world has ever known, yet he said that the pleasure he got out of reading good books was so real and so satisfying that he would rather have it than all the millions amassed by man.

This great pleasure is yours for the asking. Let's start in by reading more and better books.

Once a young man from Brooklyn wrote me a letter to talk about one of his problems. His name was Edward Murphy.

"I am very anxious to get ahead, Mr. Carnegie," he told me, "but it just seems as if I can't, no matter how hard I try. I am working as ambulance driver answering city police emergency calls. I work for twenty-four hours and then lay off for twenty-four hours. My salary is $90 a month. I'll never get a pension, no matter how long I work, and there is positively no chance of any advancement. I have been stuck in this job for seven years."

Edward was very wise in wanting to leave his present job. It was a blind alley job. There was no future to it. "If you don't study and prepare yourself now for better things," I said, "where will you be when you reach fifty? Your employer will want younger men to drive the ambulance. You will have no pension. You will be on relief."

Edward was twenty-nine years old. That's comparatively young, but I told him, "Remember that in twenty-one more years, you will be fifty. Twenty-one more years may not seem like a long time now, but it will pass with a rapidity that will leave you absolutely breathless."

Edward was married, with a baby on the way. "Mr. Carnegie," he said, "I want to be able to give that baby a good home and a college education. I don't want that baby to have to go through what I have gone through. I want to go to school and study motors and generators. But with $90 a month salary, rent to pay and a little baby coming along, I just can't afford to pay for schooling."

I suggested that he go the Brooklyn High School for Special Trades and register for a course in dynamos and motors. "When you finish with that course," I advised, "take other courses along the same line. Don't merely be content to get a better job. Why don't you aspire to make yourself a master of motors? Remember that better motors are going to be built in the next twenty years, and if you can figure out a way to do it, you can make a fortune. The man who is going to build these motors twenty years from now may not have any more ability than you have.

"You answer emergency calls, don't you? You undoubtedly spend some time sitting in the ambulance, doing nothing. Why don't you go to a public library and borrow a book on motors, keep it beside you in the ambulance, and devote every spare minute of your time to studying that book?"

When Theodore Roosevelt was in the White House, he used to have almost his entire day taken up with a series of fifteen-minute appointments, yet he kept an open book on his desk so he could read for 100 seconds between appointments. If you want to get ahead, you must learn to utilize every 100 seconds of your spare time. Remember that you are going to get out of this life exactly what you put into it. Nothing more.

# PART THREE

## *Ensure Great Interactions*

What do you think about most of the day?

Answer: yourself! Let's face it: the vast majority of us devote a great deal of our thoughts to our own concerns. All day long, we think about ourselves. A song we like comes on the radio as we drive to work; we sing along and think how the lyrics are about us. Our coworker tells us she is taking a week off next month, and we think, "I'll have to do her shift at the reception desk that week." Everything is about us.

If you want to ensure great interactions with others, just do what they do: think about them. This may seem like advice to be insincere and manipulative, but once you start this practice, you'll find that it is sincere. Others will respond to you in a way that is pleasing for you, not because you've manipulated them into it, but because they genuinely want to do so.

As you think more and more positively about yourself and develop self-understanding, determination, and confidence, you'll see that you really don't need to spend so much time thinking about yourself; thinking about others will be natural. You're going to love this new you, and so will everybody else!

# CHAPTER TWELVE

# Make a Lasting Impression

Creating a good first impression is much easier than trying later to overcome a poor one. There are three things about you that make a lasting impression on those you meet.

1. Your personal appearance: whether you are well-groomed.
2. Your manner: the poise with which you hold yourself.
3. Your speech: not only the correctness of your English, but your tone of voice.

It isn't important that you be handsome or beautiful, but you do want to be warm and affable. When you enter a room, be sure to smile. When you meet someone for the first time, make a point of finding a topic that he or she would like to talk about, and talk about that. If you don't have much expertise in that area, ask the other person questions. People enjoy sharing information about topics that interest them. If you're at a complete loss for words, offer a compliment. You can always tell someone that you like her necklace or his shoes. It's a way to break the ice, and the recipient will feel good about herself or himself. Lastly, always be positive in your statements. Negative comments may make you feel smart, but they don't make you look smart.

Today, we don't talk much about being poised, but poise is critical to gaining the respect of others. Think about your friends and the people you work with. How many people do you know who are well poised? Are you? It is surprising how many people lack poise. It is not difficult to acquire, but it never will be acquired through thinking of yourself, how you appear to others, or what impression you are making.

Years ago, President Woodrow Wilson admitted that he had despaired in his early youth of ever overcoming his self-consciousness and lack of poise. So he sat down one day and thought it out with himself. Then, when in a social or political gathering, he formed the habit of remaining quietly observant of those around him for a few seconds. This gave him an opportunity to collect himself. He realized that the important thing was to think about other people and not himself. There is nothing old-fashioned about taking the time to be quiet and listen to others.

Certain nervous affectations that may readily grow into common habits, hindering you from acquiring poise and robbing you of attractiveness. Among them are:

1. Fumbling with a string of beads or other jewelry
2. Pulling your tie
3. Smoothing your clothing
4. Checking your makeup in your pocket mirror, or putting on lipstick
5. Biting your lips or your nails
6. Drumming with your fingers
7. Tapping your feet as you sit
8. Pacing up and down the room

When you are in the presence of other people, forget about your appearance and what the others might be thinking of you. Concentrate all your thoughts on the others.

Gilbert T. Hodges, of the executive board of the *New York Sun*, lectured to thousands of young men and women on how to get ahead in business. He said, "There's no royal road to success: that there are no cut-and-dried rules that can be blindly followed. Nevertheless, I have developed a theory, which, if followed, will, I am firmly convinced, land anyone in the ranks of the successful. What I'm going to say won't be found in the textbooks, and it won't be heard in classrooms. It's too radical for that, and it will undoubtedly shock a lot of people, especially educators, for it contains lots of dynamite intended to blast away some of the mountains of bunk surrounding the subject of success."

Mr. Hodges points out that for hundreds of years, prominent men have been giving advice on how to succeed. They say you must work hard, do your duty, be honest, loyal, frugal, and have courage and energy. If you're satisfied to hold down the same job for forty years, those may be the only qualities you need. These qualities make good clerks, but they are not enough to make important executives. Someone who wants to forge ahead must have something in addition to these qualities.

"Let us begin," says Mr. Hodges, "by comparing each of us with a piece of merchandise. For that is what everyone is: just a piece of merchandise. When we came into this world, we were just raw material entering the factory of life. Our parents nursed us, molded us, and tried to make us strong and useful. They polished us off with a little education, more or less, and then offered us to the world.

"Our job now is to advertise and sell ourselves just as we would advertise and sell an automobile, a refrigerator, or a new hat. Our success in life will be measured almost entirely by how well we sell ourselves."

Mr. Hodges doesn't believe in the old saw that says if you build a better mousetrap, the world will beat a pathway to your door. "That's one of the world's greatest fallacies," he says. "For there are thousands of people who built excellent mousetraps and then went broke, because they didn't know how to sell them. No, anyone with an ambition to succeed must seek his fortune; the world will never seek him."

Mr. Hodges offers three steps for selling yourself.

*First*, you must have a meritorious product, which is yourself—what you know and what you can do. You must know our business and be able to deliver the goods when called upon.

*Second*, you must design an attractive package for yourself. You must make yourself attractive and pleasing to the world physically, mentally, and socially. Your package should be as well designed and attractive as if you were selling merchandise. A good product in a poor package won't sell; neither will you, no matter how good you are, if you are done up in a slovenly and unattractive wrapper.

This means your personal appearance, your clothes, your disposition, your health, and your manner of speech. You must cultivate an attractive and agreeable personality. A pleasing personality is not born, as many people think, but may be developed by anyone.

*Third*, you must carry on a continuous advertising and selling campaign for the purpose of keeping the merits of your merchandise favorably before the public. Success in this campaign means making favorable impressions upon all the people you come in contact with and creating the desire to employ your services.

Andrew Carnegie, who began working for 2 cents an hour and accumulated $100 million, came near the truth when he said, "Faithful and conscientious discharge of the duties assigned to you is all very well, but this alone will not do. There must be something beyond this. . . . We make clerks, bookkeepers, cashiers, bank tellers of this class, and there they remain till the end of the chapter. The rising man must do something exceptional, and beyond the range of his special department. He must attract attention."

I once asked Carnegie's associate Charles M. Schwab why he was paid a salary of several hundred thousand dollars, and whether it was because of his knowledge of steel.

He said, "No, I have forty men working for me who know far more about steel than I do."

Charles Schwab was paid his enormous salary largely because of his ability to please and influence people.

That's the game in all walks of life. For example, it's not the lawyer who knows the most law who makes the most money. The successful lawyer is the one who takes an active part in the social and economic, and perhaps political, life of the community. His knowledge goes far beyond the realm of the law, and his social relations go far beyond the limits of the courtroom and his law library. He attracts big clients and big fees.

This does not mean that in order to succeed, you must be a glad-hander, a hail-fellow-well-met, or a professional backslapper, because it simply doesn't work. It doesn't work in the selling of merchandise, and it doesn't work in selling ourselves. Sincerity is the backbone of success selling, and nothing is more fatal than transparent flattery. The more you advertise an imperfect product, the more you emphasize its defects. Likewise, the more you attract attention to yourself, the more apparent become your flaws and imperfections. By all means, you must have good merchandise, or all the selling in the world will be of no avail.

Two surveys were made on the subject of what causes people to buy. A leading institute of technology found that knowledge of the product's utility only entered into the sale to the extent of 15 percent; other factors influenced the sale to the extent of 85 percent. The head of a large business college expressed this same conclusion another way. He said that, on the average, in buying goods, we use our reason only to the extent of 15 percent, and our emotions are responsible for the other 85 percent of the transaction.

Outside of such things as potatoes and apples and beefsteaks, people take for granted the usefulness of the article, but the inspiration to buy it is prompted by such emotional appeals as style, color, design, fashion, reputation, goodwill, pride of ownership, social prestige, friendship, and the like.

Take one example: What makes woman buy a hat? Is it the quality of the material and the workmanship and the fact that it keeps the sun and the rain off her head? No, those are minor considerations. Eighty-five percent of the sale depends upon the style and lines of the hat and whether in the lady's opinion it is becoming and will add to her attractiveness.

If the percentages fixed by these experts are correct, and there is a close analogy between selling and succeeding, don't you see what a startling conclusion must be drawn? Namely, that our product—that is, what we are, what we know, and what we can do constitutes only 15 percent of the job of getting ahead. The second and third steps, that is, the packaging and the sales campaign, are the big guns in getting ahead in life, and count for 85 percent of the battle.

There are many ways to develop your power to please, convince, and persuade people. You should have a wide range of knowledge so that you can talk with all kinds of people about the things that interest them rather than what interests you. Also, the ability to converse intelligently on the important topics of the day will be a mighty factor in your efforts to please people.

Now that you've got something to say, it's most important to say it well. That means learning to speak well, both in public and in private. More jobs and sales are lost through an inability to express one's ideas and thoughts than through any other single cause.

The final step in putting these advantages to work is to keep yourself in circulation. It is fatal to be a miser with your talents. You should make as many contacts are possible. Take an active part in the social, economic, and political life of your community. In this way, you will meet influential people who will naturally be attracted to your sound ability and pleasing personality. Don't hide your light under a bushel. Hold it high so all the world may see that it is burning brightly.

Let's sum up the previous points.

For getting ahead in life, your knowledge and ability will enter into the struggle only to the extent of 15 percent.

Your ability to sell yourself by meeting and mingling with others, by pleasing people and winning them to your way of thinking, will constitute 85 percent of the battle. You can do this not by insincerity, flattery, or meaningless handshaking, but by improving the mind, cultivating a pleasing personality, a cheerful disposition, and a good appearance, and having a genuine, unselfish interest in other people and their problems.

Try this approach. It will work miracles.

# CHAPTER THIRTEEN

# Smile: The Next Rule of Success

The impact of smiling is so dramatic that it's worth devoting an entire chapter to it. If you want people to like you, one of the best ways to do it is by smiling. Now let's make one thing very clear. I am not talking about a silly, forced, insincere grin. That doesn't fool anybody except the person who is doing it. I am talking about a smile that just wells up from inside of you. I am talking about an old-fashioned, tail-wagging smile. When a puppy wags his tail, he says, "I am glad to see you." When you smile, you say the same thing. If you are glad to see me, I am going to be glad to see you.

Stockbroker William Steinhardt came to me for help a few years ago. He wanted to make people like him. He had been married for eighteen years, and yet he confessed to me that during all that time he had seldom smiled at his wife or spoken two dozen words to her from the time he got up in the morning until he left for his office. I suggested to him that he try smiling at people for a week. This is what happened.

"The next morning when I got up," he said, "I looked at my sorry mug in the mirror while combing my hair and I said to myself, 'Bill, you are going to wipe the scowl off that sour puss of yours today. You are going to smile. And you are going to begin right now.' As I sat down to breakfast, I greeted my wife with a 'Good morning, my dear,' and smiled as I said it.

"She didn't know what to make of it. She hadn't seen a smile on my face at that time of the day in ten years. She was shocked! I told her she could expect a smiling face every morning,

"This changed attitude of mine has brought more happiness in my home than anything else in the world. When I smile, I feel better myself. I have got the habit of doing it now. When I leave for work in the morning, I greet the elevator boy in the apartment house with a 'Good morning.' I greet the doorman with a smile. I smile at the man in the subway booth when I ask him for change. I smile at people who come to me with complaints on the floor of the stock exchange. I find that smiles are bringing me more happiness and dollars every day of my life."

Everybody in the world is seeking happiness, and there is one sure way to find it: by controlling your thoughts. Happiness doesn't depend on outward conditions. It depends on inner conditions. It isn't what you have, who you are, where you are, or what you are doing that makes you happy or unhappy. It is what you think about it. For example, I have seen two people in the same place, doing the same thing, each of them with about equal amounts of money and prestige, and yet one was miserable and the other happy. Why? Because each one had a different mental attitude.

"Nothing is good or bad," said Shakespeare, "but thinking makes it so." So let's make smile our how to win rule in our lives. Nothing insincere, mind you. It must be real. It must come right from the heart.

The next time you need to phone a customer service office, try smiling throughout the call. When you smile, the tenor of your voice changes; you convey that you are warm and happy. The person on the other end will hear the upbeat tone of your voice, and there's a good chance that he or she will more helpful to you than if you had spoken harshly or even neutrally.

# CHAPTER FOURTEEN

# Develop a Winning Personality

Yes, it is axiomatic that people gravitate toward those who are pleasant to them, yet this fact does not seem to actually affect the behavior of many people. Experience shows, however, that in the world of day-to-day interactions, being pleasant is the way to get what you want. Let's say that you want to return an item to a store. Do you expect the clerk to happily take the item back if you make your request in a way that is surly or demanding? You're much more likely to have a smooth transaction if you are polite and kind. Similarly, being pleasant at work is the way to get people to work happily with you and the way to get ahead. We want to please those who appreciate us and act respectfully toward us. No one wants to spend the day with a bully or work for a boss who is condescending and unreasonable. That person will constantly be looking for new employees, which is not a recipe for success.

I spoke to Mr. Ernest Lawton, personnel director of Macy's, the biggest department store in the world, and asked him for advice on how to sell our services to an employer.

In the course of a year, Mr. Lawton and his associates interviewed about 150,000 applicants for jobs at Macy's. That's about one tenth. In other words, out of every ten persons who applied for work, only one was hired. I asked him what was wrong with the other nine.

"As a rule," he said, "they fall down on our very first requirement: personality. That's the first thing we look for. In fact, our first interview with an applicant is to size up his personality. If a person can sell us on their personality in a interview of a few minutes, we're pretty sure they can sell the customer too. Because, you see, getting a job is really a selling proposition. The individual looking for a job has something to sell just as definitely as Macy's has. We sell merchandise, but what has the individual to sell? Themselves, their personality, their services, and their capacity for work. Just as we have to present out merchandise in an effective manner, so the individual has to present themselves in an effective manner. That's salesmanship."

When I asked Mr. Lawton what exactly he meant by personality, he replied, "How a person talks. Do they speak sincerely and convincingly? Do they have character? Do they show confidence? Not overconfidence—I don't mean that—but are they sure of themselves in a simple, direct way? When they speak, do they talk in a natural, well-modulated voice? What is their manner? Are they pleasing in their manner? Do they smile in a friendly way? Do they dress well? And by that I don't mean whether they wear expensive clothing or dress in the latest style. We realize that people looking for work usually can't afford new clothes, but they can afford to be neat and clean and well pressed. All these things— voice, manner, speech, smile, character, and clothes— are part of personality. We can train our employees. It's the material a person has that counts most, and how they present it. What do they have to build on?"

Mr. Lawton added that of the 150,000 he and his staff interview, about one out of five passed the test for personality. That didn't mean they couldn't develop it; it only means that they hadn't yet learned how to do so.

"Next to personality, I look for ambition," added Mr. Lawton. "At our second interview, we ask a lot of what may seem like foolish questions, like, 'Why did you leave school before you finished?' or 'Why did you leave your previous job?' We're really trying to find out whether or not they know where they are going in their own private lives. If they have used good judgment in their own affairs, they are likely to use good judgment in ours. When we hire a person—man or woman, executive or sales clerk—we have in mind the idea of promotion. Even when we hire a stockroom clerk of seventeen, we try to figure out what they going to be at twenty-one."

Next, he added, "in an organization as big as Macy's, we need people who can get along with the other 25,000 employees. It takes self-control to get along with all sorts of people. If you have ideas, you have to be able to sell them to the person. All along the line, it's salesmanship.

"How can a person applying for a job convince me that he or she has ideas? Well, an alert person with ideas who walked around our store with their eyes open could probably see a half-dozen places open to improvement. Now suppose a young man or a young woman looked over our store and then applied for a job with a concrete suggestion for improving our methods in even one department. We might not act upon the suggestion, for there might be a dozen practical reasons why we could not, but one thing at least is certain: if that idea is a good one and shows real business sense, we'd know that that person has ideas. More important still, we'd realize right away that they see things from our point of view."

In short, Mr. Lawton's advice to applicants is, first, develop your personality. In other words, learn to speak sincerely and convincingly, and in a natural and easy voice. Smile in a pleasant and friendly manner. Dress as well as you can within your means, and above all in a suitable manner. And show your employer that you have ideas to apply to their business.

Mr. Lawton also offers another point to remember: "Brains are a lot cheaper and easier to use than shoe leather. One hour's serious thought will give you more results for your trouble than a week's running around town. You may not be looking for a job in a department store; perhaps you're just looking for a job of any kind and don't know what you're best suited for. In that case, choose a vocation, size up your past experience, then go after that job in an intelligent way.

"If you had a product to sell, you wouldn't dream of rushing in to a man and trying to sell him without any idea of what you were going to say, would you? Yet that's exactly what most people do about jobs. People almost never come to employment managers with a clearly prepared statement of what they have to offer. They wait for the employers to dig it out of them question by question, like the third degree. And employers are buyers: they're in the market to buy, provided you have something to sell, and that something is you. Therefore visualize yourself as a product. Find out why someone should invest in you, and present yourself in the best package possible."

Note that an employer is more often attuned to a candidate's personality than to his or her experience. Of course, chances are that we won't get an interview in the first place if the job is not in line with our experience. That said, of those who meet the criteria in terms of skills and training, it is hard to resist hiring the most likable person of the group. If you think back about a time when you had to choose one person from a group of individuals—perhaps for a job or a team of some sort—you may be willing to admit that you selected the most pleasant person, the one who you wanted to spend time with.

Let me repeat: if you are in business, your ability to win friends and influence people is almost six times as important in the battle for success as superior knowledge.

I once spoke before a boot and shoe convention in Chicago. A man sitting beside me at the speaker's table said he never had graduated from high school, yet for years he had a man working for him who graduated from two different colleges. In spite of his lack of formal education, the man who had not graduated from high school had a salary that was five times as large as the college man's. The college man had spent thousands of dollars to obtain a formal education. In the academic sense, he was brilliant, yet he was a failure in business and finally lost his job, just because he had not learned how to deal with people.

The ability to deal with people is not something you can learn in college. It is something you must practice every day of your life. It is, in fact, a new way of life that requires constant vigilance, constant practice, and constant application.

For years, I've been working almost every night in the first and only laboratory of human relations that has ever existed: the Dale Carnegie Institute. In this laboratory, I've dealt with countless thousands of men and women, and I have often found that the highly skilled workman is the hardest to convince of the importance of dealing with people. People who know their work thoroughly are apt to say, "Oh, that stuff's all nonsense. I don't have to bother making people like me to hold down a job, as long as I do my work well."

One man used to say that very thing. He was an optician: a skilled workman in a difficult and highly specialized craft. His name was Joseph Duffee, and he lived on Long Island.

"I grind eyeglasses for spectacles," he said. "I worked for twelve years for one firm in Boston. I had seven men working under me, and when I didn't like the way they did things, I just told them so. If the boss asked me why work wasn't out on time, I simply told him if he didn't like the way I was running things, he could get another man."

Mr. Duffee even fought with his boss. "I wasn't taking anything from anybody. I felt I didn't have to. Then, during the Depression, I got a pay cut, and I didn't get it back. That made me so sore that I started taking it out on everyone. But the payoff came one week when I was out a day and got docked for it. I got so mad I grabbed my pay envelope, barged straight into the boss's office without so much as knocking, and threw the envelope in his face.

"'I've been docked one-day's pay,' I said.

"'You were out one day, weren't you?'

"'You've never docked anyone around here before. Why pick on me?'

"'You weren't sick, were you?'

"'You know I wasn't sick; I had business I had to attend to. You're quick enough to cut my salary when times are tough, but I notice you're not so quick in giving it back to me when times are better. I've worked for you for twelve years, and you docked me for one day's pay. You wouldn't do that to anyone else around here.'

"'You're right, Duffee,' said my boss. 'I wouldn't do it to anyone else. But you've got it coming to you.'

"'What do you mean—coming to me?'

"'You've had your little say. Now I'm going to tell you a thing or two. You're a troublemaker, Duffee. Nobody likes you. And what's more, you're the kind of a foreman that gets the men to fighting among themselves. I'm sick of it. And the only reason I've put up with your arrogant attitude these twelve years . . .'

"'Is because I'm the only man around here who really knows his job!'

"'You're right again, Duffee. You're the best we've got, but you've got such a mean, ornery, streak in you.'

"'What are you paying me for—soft soap and backslapping? You're paying me for first-class work, and that's what you're getting. I want to be paid for that day I was out!'

"'Oh, you want to be paid for the day you were out! Well, from now on, you're going to be out every day! I don't care if you're the best workman on God's green earth, I've put up with you just as long as I can stand it! You're fired!'

"'So I'm fired!" I said. 'OK! Give me that pay envelope! I'm not worried. I can get another job any time.'

"But I didn't, and I had a wife and five children to support. One day one of the biggest opticians in Boston sent for me; I thought it meant a job at last. But he just called me there to bawl me out.

"He told me I was going to be out of work a long time. My reputation had traveled before me. They all knew I was a good workman, but they wouldn't take a chance on a troublemaker. He said I'd never get another job as long as I wore that chip on my shoulder."

Mr. Duffee was out of work for three months. "I used up all my savings, and then a friend of mine got me a job in New York. But I still hadn't learned my lesson. I just thought I'd got a raw deal.

"It started out to be the same story. I had several spats with the new boss's son and told him where to get off."

Then Mr. Duffee read my book *How to Win Friends and Influence People*. "It made me think," he said, "and for the first time the idea filtered through my skull that if I kept on antagonizing people, I'd be just another good workman looking for a job for the rest of my life.

"First I began to work hard at controlling my temper. It wasn't easy, but I found out if I could just hold my tongue for five minutes, I was safe. After five minutes, I didn't even feel like blowing up."

This change made a big difference in Mr. Duffee's life. He told me, "Two months later the boss called me in and said, 'Duffee, I don't like the way the shop is being run. I wish you'd take charge and see what you can do.'"

Mr. Duffee became a foreman again. "And then I really did put those principles to work: instead of bawling the men out or criticizing them when their work wasn't right, I'd praise what they did well and show them tactfully how to correct their bad work."

To Mr. Duffee's own amazement, his boss called him in and congratulated him on the job he was doing. And when Christmas arrived, he received a substantial raise in pay. What's more, Mr. Duffee's old boss in Boston heard about the change that had come over him and wrote a letter congratulating him and wishing him luck.

Mr. Duffee used this changed attitude outside of the office as well. "I have three times as many friends as I ever had before," he said. "I am now helping to organize a social club in my hometown, and also a consumers' cooperative store. I used to enjoy a good fight, but now I get ten times as much excitement and happiness out of working with people."

There is an old and true saying to the effect that you get out of life just what you put into it. It is also true that your attitude toward other people will determine their attitude toward you. Woodrow Wilson once said, "If you come at me with your fists doubled, I think I can promise you that mine will double as fast as yours." That's human nature, and it's true of all of us. If you go at people day after day with your fists doubled, and with an aggressive, belligerent, disgruntled attitude, other people will have precisely that same attitude toward you.

For example, take the case of Sir Richard Burton, the nineteenth-century explorer who was one of the most gifted men the British Empire ever produced. He was in government service, and like Lawrence of Arabia, he went in disguise among the Arabs. Sir Richard Burton was one of the first Christians who ever made the forbidden and dangerous pilgrimage to the Muslim holy city of Mecca. He performed the incredible feat of mastering over forty languages and dialects, and he translated *The Arabian Nights* into English. He was one of the most brilliant scholars who ever lived. He served his country faithfully and well on many dangerous missions. No other man of his day was more deserving of great honors. But did he get the recognition and promotions he deserved? No! Why? Because with all his brilliance he could not get along with other people, and he persisted in antagonizing his superiors, which ruined his career.

The late John D. Rockefeller said, "I will pay more for the ability to deal with people than for any other ability under the sun." Many a person is a failure simply because they lack this ability.

Abraham Lincoln once said, "If you would win a man to your cause, first convince him with sincerity that you are his true friend. Therein is a drop of honey that catches his heart; which, say what you will, is the great high road to his reason."

So let us take this how to win rule from Abraham Lincoln: if you would win a person to your cause, first convince them that you are their true friend. There is no greater secret of how to succeed.

Let us now look into what it takes to be a likable boss.

You know very few of us see ourselves as others see us. So the best way to find out what people think of us is to ask the other fellow. For example, ask the average secretary what she thinks of her boss. Her estimate isn't just limited to the office: the boss acts the same wherever he is—at home, at the club, or out among his customers.

So what a secretary thinks of the man she works for is what other people think of him too. You may not be a boss, or a secretary, but the principles I am going to discuss here will help you realize why people like you or dislike you, regardless of whether you are a banker or a barber or a chauffeur or a mother.

What do secretaries think of the men they work for? The Katharine Gibbs School, one of the largest secretarial schools in America, with branches in New York, Boston, and Providence, sent out a confidential questionnaire to more than a thousand secretaries from coast to coast.

In the answers to this questionnaire, neither the secretaries nor the firms for which they worked would ever be made public. I wasn't shown the question-naires, but I was given ten pages of typewritten material summarizing what these women liked and didn't like about their employers. I was so intrigued by this information that I went out and interviewed a number of secretaries myself.

One secretary said, "I dislike my boss because he is a sourpuss. He usually comes down to the office with a grouch on. He never smiles. He never asks me how I am feeling. Sometimes he doesn't even say, 'Good morning.' He hurts my feelings by barking orders at me when other people are around. He doesn't hand me work to do. He throws it at me."

This secretary can be grateful for one thing: that she is this man's secretary and not his wife. Can you imagine what that man does to his family when he gets home? An old Chinese proverb says, "A man who doesn't smile shouldn't keep a shop." And he shouldn't be a boss either. Old-fashioned cheerfulness is a priceless asset, both in business and social life.

For example, I sometimes have breakfast at a large restaurant on 42nd Street. There are over a dozen servers in that restaurant, but two of them stand out above all the others. Why? Because they are always smiling. They radiate welcome and good nature. They make my breakfast a ceremony of morning cheerfulness. Is it any wonder that I always make it a point to sit at the table served by one of those two people? They give me no better service than anyone else, and they bring me the same food. But they do it with such good spirit that the same food actually tastes better.

The first rule for how to avoid getting yourself generally disliked: if you want to be popular, don't be a sourpuss.

Another secretary told me what she disliked about her boss: "I dislike the fact that I never get home on time. He makes me work overtime almost every night. I wouldn't mind if it were really necessary, but it isn't. He hates to dictate letters, so he puts off dictating his mail until after four o'clock. Then I have to stay till six-thirty or seven at night to get the letters typed. I know he means well, but he is just thoughtless."

There are lots of people like that. They never think about what other people want. They think only of what they want. And these people are never popular. For example, I was having dinner with some friends not long ago. There were eight people present. One man wanted to go down in the basement and play ping-pong, although nobody else had the slightest interest in playing. But did that faze him? No sir, he kept on insisting until finally all of us had to go down to the basement and watch him play. We all secretly hoped we would never be invited to a dinner party again where he was.

If you want to be popular, rule two is: consider other people's desires and wishes. Don't insist on doing only what you want to do.

A third secretary said she liked her present boss, but previously, "I used to work for a large publishing house. I worked every Sunday and took Mondays off. I dropped in to my office one Monday to get something on my desk, and the publisher asked me if I would write four or five letters for him. That wasn't my job, but naturally I said, 'Yes, I'd be glad to do it.' He didn't dictate the letters; he simply gave me the gist of what he wanted to say.

"There were personal letters, letters to friends of his. I took the letters to his desk. Do you think he bothered to thank me for taking time from my day off to do him a favor? No. He merely read the letters through, signed them, then threw them back at me and said, 'Mail them.' That man's a big shot in the publishing world, but I'd hate to tell you just how small he is in my estimation. What's more, that happened seven or eight years ago, and I'm still sore about it."

Now contrast that man with Owen D. Young, chairman of the board of the General Electric Company. Owen D. Young was getting off a Pullman sleeper in Florida.

He had had an enjoyable and restful trip from New York, and the Pullman porter had been courteous and attentive. Owen D. Young gave him a generous tip and said, "I wish I could always be sure of doing my job as perfectly as you do yours."

Did Mr. Young mean what he said? Of course he meant it. No man handling the complex and confounding problems that Mr. Young wrestled with could even hope to come as near to perfection as that porter did.

Mr. Young's words of appreciation did four things. First, they made the porter happy. Second, because they made the porter happy, they also gave Mr. Young a feeling of satisfaction. Third, they inspired the porter to want to continue to do a splendid job. And fourth, they impressed me so much I am telling them to you. I hope that this will move you to give a few extra words of appreciation tomorrow.

So if you want to be popular, rule three is: don't forget to say, "Thank you." Don't treat your employees as if they were so many slaves.

Another secretary told me, "My boss is always complaining, always telling everybody how hard he works, how tired he is, and how nobody appreciates all he does. He goes around saying, 'I'm the neck of the bottle. Everything has to come out of me. Why can't somebody else do something right for a change? Why do I have to be driven crazy?'"

That man was affected with the devastating disease of self-pity. He should have remembered there are only four persons on earth who are interested in hearing about your troubles: your mother, your preacher, your doctor, and your lawyer. And your doctor and your lawyer are paid for listening to your troubles.

I spoke once with the Reverend Oliver M. Butterfield in New York City, one of the foremost authorities on marriage in America, who devoted years to studying the causes of marital disasters. I asked Dr. Butterfield about self-pity, having a martyr complex, and blaming everybody but yourself. I asked him how much they had to do with divorce. He said that self-pity was a tremendously important factor in divorce.

So if you want to be popular, rule four is: don't go around pitying yourself and whining about your troubles.

A fifth secretary told me, "I have got a terrible boss. He is so conceited. Nobody likes him. He is always talking about how important he is, how he's the world's best writer of advertising copy. Why, I actually heard him say once in a public talk that he had always been successful in everything he had ever undertaken. He is always belittling other people and bragging about the great things he is going to do."

The famous philosopher Sir Francis Bacon said that when a man falls in love with himself, it is generally the beginning of a lifelong romance. This lady's boss reminds me of General John Pope. During the

Civil War, Lincoln put General Pope in charge of the Army of the Potomac. Pope immediately issued a proclamation to the army bragging about all the victories he had won in the West, and he insinuated that the soldiers on the Potomac were a lot of cowards. Mind you, he actually condemned the soldiers who were expected to fight for him, and then boasted about the entire military miracles he was going to perform. He issued so many bombastic announcements he was soon called "Proclamation Pope."

What happened? Pope's officers and men despised him. He was about as popular as a diamondback rattlesnake. Now that happened many years ago. But I'll bet there is hardly a business in America that hasn't at some time or another had its little "Proclamation Pope," bragging about the miracles he's about to perform.

So here is rule five: if you want people to like you, don't go around bragging about how smart you are and telling other people about your brilliant achievements.

I hope I haven't given the impression that all secretaries dislike their bosses, for I was very much impressed by the number of secretaries who talked at length about what they liked in the men they worked for.

Now let's summarize the five points brought out by the five secretaries I have just mentioned. If you want to be popular not only with your secretary, but with your wife, your child, your sweetheart, and everybody else, here's the way to do it:

**1. Don't be a sourpuss.** Smile. Radiate cheerfulness, and people will be glad to see you come in and sorry to see you leave.

**2. Consider other people's desires and wishes.** Don't insist on doing only what you want to do.

**3. Never take favors for granted.** Always say thank you, and people will go out of their way to serve you.

**4. Don't go around pitying yourself and whining about your troubles.** Remember other people have tribulations too.

**5. Don't go around telling people how smart you are and bragging about your brilliant achievements.** Let other people find out for themselves what a great person you are.

These rules of behavior may seem simplistic, but it's surprising how infrequently we adhere to them. Ask yourself, how often do I take my girlfriend to see a thriller when I know that she'd like a comedy better? How often do I beg my coworkers to have lunch with me at the Indian place, even though they aren't that crazy about Indian food? Do I take the time to let people know that I'm grateful for their efforts on my behalf? Do I follow these rules for success and give honest, sincere appreciation, or do I just expect others to do things for me? Do I inflict my problems on people? Do I often tell my spouse or friends about what a bad day I had, or how stupid my boss is, or how much my neck hurts from the stress I carry there?

Many of us do these things without thinking about them, but they don't make for a positive experience for those around us. It's much more enjoyable to be with someone who asks us about ourselves, smiles, and is pleasant.

# CHAPTER FIFTEEN

# Show Your Thoughtfulness

Wouldn't you like to have people like you better? Wouldn't you like to have more friends? If you're in business, wouldn't you like to have people travel out of their way just for the pleasure of doing business with you?

The only purpose of this chapter is to show you how you can accomplish all these things. Sounds like a big order, doesn't it? Yet we have received scores of letters from people who are achieving such results by applying the principles described here. You can use and profit by them regardless of whether you are a homemaker, a salesman, an executive, a clerk, a doctor, or a schoolteacher.

Mr. F. H. Drake ran the Atlantic filling station in Huntingdon, Pennsylvania, a town with a population of 8,500.

At one point, Mr. Drake was watching his business die. "Filling stations were springing up all around me like weeds. Everybody was cutting prices, and then of course winter is the worst time for filling stations in small towns.

"I called on my friends and acquaintances and asked them to give me their business, and I advertised in the newspapers every week. When January came, I got panicky, because in my part of the country, January is the worst month of the year for selling gasoline. Lots of cars are laid up waiting for new license plates, and naturally there are not many tourists. We always expect a slump of about 15 percent in January."

When you are barely making expenses, a slump of 15 percent may prove disastrous.

Mr. Drake tuned into my radio program one night and bought *How to Win Friends and Influence People.* "I made up my mind always to listen to the program after that," he said, "and one night, I heard a grocer from Staten Island say he sent letters to his customers. I decided to try the same idea in my business too. So I began writing letters to everyone who bought my gas or oil. About a third of my business comes from credit cards, and I got the names from them, or I copied down the license numbers and got the names and addresses from the license bureau at the state capital.

"In these letters, I told each person how grateful I was for the business they gave me, and, believe you me, I was grateful. I told them it was a pleasure to serve them—and it was. I told them I hoped to have that pleasure again sometime—and I meant it.

"What happened almost took my breath away. By golly, I was so surprised. If I had not seen the results with my own eyes, I would not have believed them. I had only been doing this for about two months, and people as far away as Philadelphia, Pittsburgh, Harrisburg, and Elmira began coming back regularly for more gas and oil and greeted me like an old friend. Many of them told me that my letter was the first time anybody had ever thought enough of their business to write and say thank you. One man drove in from Altoona, Pennsylvania, and he said, 'Well, I got your letter and I just wanted to say hello. I have enough gas to get home on, but fill 'er up anyway.'"

One customer drove to Huntington each week on business. This man used to buy his gas in his hometown, but after getting that letter, he would drive past fifty cut-rate filling stations to buy his gas from Mr. Drake. And he paid 2 cents a gallon more for it—all because of Mr. Drake's letters of thanks.

"Not only that," says Mr. Drake, "but a man from Harrisburg drove into my station the other day. He had noticed he was low on gas when he was back in

Lewistown, which is thirty-five miles away, and he was afraid he might have to stop to buy gas from someone else on the way. He told me he almost held his breath during the last few miles for fear his car would stop before he got to my station. And he was a stranger. I had only seen him once before.

"I just couldn't believe it. What has happened has made me dizzy. I never knew I could do such things. Things are certainly running smoothly now."

If you want to get ahead in business, if you want to increase your income, if you want people to like you, do unselfish little things for them and be more courteous. Charles Schwab once told me a story that strikingly illustrates the value of courtesy. He said that one afternoon the clerks in one of New York's largest department stores were chatting among themselves when a customer entered. It was raining outside, and the customer, a woman, was wet and uncomfortable. Did any of the salespeople pay any attention to her? Yes, one young man did. His name was Alexander Peacock. He asked her what he could do to serve her, and after he had waited on her, he escorted her to the door, got an umbrella, and took her to a taxicab. Just before the cab drove off, the woman said, "Have you a card? I want to know your name."

A few months later, that same department store received an order for a large shipment of goods to furnish a castle in Scotland. Accompanying the order was the request that this particular young clerk, Alexander Peacock, should accompany the shipment to Scotland and help install it.

The store was astonished. The management protested. This clerk, they pointed out, was one of their youngest men. Why not send someone with years of experience, an expert? No, the customer refused to accept anyone else, so this young man was sent across the Atlantic to Scotland in charge of one of the biggest orders in the store's history.

That unknown woman he had escorted to the door and put into a taxicab happened to be the wife of one of the richest men who ever lived. She happened to be the wife of Andrew Carnegie. That clerk's life was changed by a little act of courtesy. A simple act of courtesy may well prove to be the turning point in your career too.

I'll bet there are thousands of readers who are saying this very second, "I know I ought to be more courteous. I ought to say thank people more often." But merely knowing that you ought to do it won't help you at all unless you really do something about it. Most of us need to develop the habit of being more courteous. And to develop a new, good habit requires constant thought and daily effort.

So tomorrow let's all start to be more courteous. Let's get into the habit of using such phrases as these:

"I'm awfully sorry to trouble you. Would you be so kind as to do such and such? I appreciate your thoughtfulness. I thank you." And so on. I once saw a sign above a cigar counter in a hotel in South Bend, Indiana, that read: "Your money back if we forget to say thank you."

Mind you, a mere mechanical expression of thanks won't do any good. It has to come right from the heart. It has to be real. For example, years ago I was living in Paris, trying to learn to write. I got my own breakfast in my room each morning. I bought orange marmalade from a small neighborhood grocery. When the marmalade glass was empty, I would take it back and buy another jar of marmalade. That happened years ago, but I still remember the thrill I got in buying that marmalade.

I was greeted with bubbling enthusiasm: "Ah, Monsieur!" How had I been? How was my book coming along? Did I enjoy the marmalade? Honestly, I could hardly have gotten more attention if I had been the president of France! That little Frenchman and his wife made every occasion a real occasion. They showed me how much they appreciated my patronage, and I was so pleased that I would gladly have walked ten blocks out of my way to do business with them.

Think about ways you might be more thoughtful of others. Do you return your doorman's smile? Do you thank your assistant at the office for doing a good job? How about always being on time? It might seem that such everyday things should be a given, but if, for example, your assistant is often late, his or her timeliness will start to feel like an issue. Everyone likes to be appreciated and to feel valued. A little courtesy and thoughtfulness is a great way to make sure that those around you know that you're aware of the gifts that they bring. As a bonus, they're bound to act courteously and thoughtfully toward you.

# CHAPTER SIXTEEN

# Think about Others and Provide Them with What They Want

A great way to be highly regarded by others is to consider and provide for their desires. This practice might be regarded as an extension of being courteous, but it is more than having good manners and being attentive. It is putting ourselves in someone else's shoes and contemplating what would make that person happy or more at ease, or what would make his or her job easier.

Years ago, a young man stood on the banks of the Chicago River. He was out of a job. All the money he had in the world was 4 cents. "Here's where I start all over again," he said, and he flung his last 4 cents in the river. Later that man became a millionaire. His name was Charles R. Walgreen, founder of the popular chain of drugstores.

Until he was thirty-five years old, Walgreen was pounding pills and jerking sodas in drugstores around Chicago. At sixty-three, he was the head of a chain of 518 drugstores scattered from coast to coast.

Once I spent a day at Mr. Walgreen's country home. We flew out from Chicago to Dixon, Illinois. There, in the identical cabin where Abe Lincoln was once entertained, I spent hours talking to Charlie Walgreen, trying to analyze his success.

Time and again, I've said that there are no cut-and-dried rules for success. Charles Walgreen's career is a striking illustration of that. He told me he never had much ambition and certainly never had any vision of what was going to happen in the future.

Mr. Walgreen also admitted that he never worked very hard, and he still doesn't work very hard. Now I've read hundreds of biographies, and interviewed hundreds of successful men. I know that ninety-nine times out of a hundred, the person who gets ahead is the person who is fired up with sleepless ambition and a passion for work. But let's be honest! Charles Walgreen is an exception to the rule.

For example, no sensible person would tell people to get angry in business. And yet if Charles Walgreen hadn't gotten angry, he probably wouldn't have become head of a chain of drugstores. In fact, his anger was the turning point in his whole life.

At the time he was an indifferent, irresponsible young clerk in a Chicago drugstore. One day a lady came in for a glass of Vichy water. Walgreen gave it to her in a glass he'd washed in sodium bicarbonate. But he hadn't dried it thoroughly, and there was a little film of sodium bicarbonate still on the glass. The customer took one look, marched over to the manager, and gave his clerk the business. What did he mean by serving her Vichy water in a dirty glass?

Now the manager knew the glass wasn't dirty. But did he explain that to the customer? No. He laid all the blame on his clerk, Charles Walgreen. He bawled him out and told him he ought to be fired. Walgreen was indignant: his precious pride was hurt. He'd show that manager a thing or two. He'd get even with him! He'd quit!

As soon as the woman left, Charlie walked to the back of the store to tell his employer he was going to quit. But his boss had already left for lunch. That gave Charlie a little time to think. He said, "If I quit now, it won't make the boss mad. I'm so darn worthless, he'd probably be glad if I quit. I know what I'll do. I'll make myself the best drugstore clerk in Chicago, and then I'll quit. Then he'll be sorry. He'll beg me to stay. But I'll tell him to take his old drugstore and jump in the lake."

That sounded like a grand idea, so he immediately sprang to life. He washed and polished all the glasses. He waited on the customers with enthusiasm. He was on the jump from morning to night. When Saturday night rolled around, he got the surprise of his life. The boss said, "Charlie, what's happened to you? Great Scott, I believe you're the best drugstore clerk in Chicago. I'm going to raise your salary $10 a month." Now Charlie was only getting $35 a month, and that $10 raise looked pretty big. So instead of quitting, he decided to stay. Not only was he getting an increase in pay, he was getting something even more important: he was now finding joy in his work. For the first time in his life, he experienced the thrill of a job well done. So he decided he would stay in the drugstore business.

Years later, when that same druggist wanted to sell his store, he gave Charlie Walgreen the first opportunity to buy it. So Walgreen borrowed $2,000, made his first down payment, and became a full-fledged drugstore owner.

Still, Charlie showed no signs of ambition. True, he had studied nights to become a registered pharmacist, and he'd read a great deal. In fact, he'd always read a great deal. As a boy he used to devour Ruskin, Bacon, and Shakespeare. Even later in life, he usually read three books at a time: a novel, a biography, and a good old-fashioned detective story.

Charles Walgreen told me that when he was operating his first drugstore, he never had the slightest idea that he would ever own another one. In fact, he took only a casual interest in his first store. Many an afternoon he would run out to a ball game, and he'd spend his evenings shooting pool. He made a bare living out of his first store. Then a friend of his, who also owned a drugstore, got in a tight place. He had to sell his store, and he begged Charlie to buy it. Now Walgreen didn't want that store. But he bought it, primarily because he wanted to help out his friend. Soon he found that if he hired the proper help, it was almost as easy to run two drugstores as one. Later on, he bought his third, and his fourth, and so it went until he had over five hundred.

I may have given the impression that Charles Walgreen is more lackadaisical than he really is. The fact is, initiative has always been one of his chief assets. For example, I told you how he sat on the banks of the Chicago River and threw his last 4 cents in the water. The next day he landed a job in a drugstore. But the druggist wanted somebody who could speak German. Charles couldn't speak a word of German. But he had initiative! He told the druggist if he'd only give him a chance, he'd learn to speak German. So he bought a German textbook and devoted every spare minute to studying the language. At the end of the first week, he was speaking German so well that the druggist amazed him by paying $8 a week when he had agreed only to pay him $7.

Another secret of Walgreen's success was his ability to think in terms of the other person's wants. As an example, when he was faced with the problem of managing his first drugstore, he got right down to brass tacks. "What do people want?" he asked himself. And he decided that people want three things: good merchandise at a reasonable price, convenience, and friendly, courteous service. Upon these three things Charles Walgreen made a fortune.

Walgreen prided himself in his ability to give prompt service. For example, when a customer down the block phoned in an order, Charlie would repeat it. In fact, he'd repeat it so loud that his clerk could hear him. Then the clerk would start getting the order together. As soon as it was all wrapped up, out dashed the clerk to the customer's house. In the meantime, Walgreen kept his customer hanging on the phone. He'd chat about her health, her children, all sorts of things to keep her interested. All at once, the woman's doorbell would ring. She'd say, "Excuse me, Mr. Walgreen, but there's someone at the door." That would make Charlie Walgreen chuckle, because he knew that it was his own clerk delivering the order. Can you imagine what a hit that made?

No, Charlie Walgreen was never afraid to try new things. In fact, business writers insist he's largely responsible for the development of the modern drugstore. The streamlined fountain, broad aisles, and brightly lit counter displays all followed in the wake of Charlie Walgreen's innovations. He made millions of children happy by making toys an all-year commodity instead of a seasonal luxury. And he transformed the old-fashioned soda fountain into a bright and pleasant lunching place—thus changing the noonday habits of working people of the nation.

Although Charles Walgreen became head of a major drugstore chain, he wouldn't have been able to get a job in Hollywood playing the part of a big businessman, because he didn't look like a go-getter. In fact, he wasn't. He was the son of a Swedish farmer. He spent his childhood on the farm, and later in life he still looked like a farmer. If I introduced you to him and told you that he was a dairy farmer, you'd never doubt it for one minute. He was modest, kindly, unassuming.

I wish you could see his office in Chicago, because I think it shows what kind of man he is. It was a small office. The day I was there, a roaring fire crackled in the fireplace. Walgreen took his little Boston bulldog to his office every day, and when I was there, the dog was playing with a ball in front of the fireplace. On the wall hung a motto that explains a great deal of Charlie Walgreen's success. It says, "They are great only who are kind." Did he put that motto on the wall? Not at all. Some of his employees bought that motto, framed it, and hung it on the wall because they knew that represented his philosophy.

I believe Charles Walgreen's personality had a lot to do with his success. I talked to a number of his employees. They loved the man, and when they told me they loved him, I knew they meant it. What's more, after you spent a day in Charlie Walgreen's home, you understood why. He was tremendously interested in serving others. "We gain helping others," he told me. "But only if we do it unselfishly, without any thought of gain."

Now I may be wrong—I frequently am—but my guess would be that that sentence does more to explain the success of Charlie Walgreen and his drugstore than any other thing I can think of.

When I left him, I asked Charles Walgreen to give me a bit of advice to pass along to you. "There are no rules for success," he said; "success is made up of steps. Make up your mind that you can do your job just as well as anybody else, and even better. Then keep your eyes and ears open. But be prepared for your opportunity. It will come. The trouble with most people is that they are like a nervous baseball player. They fight the ball instead of waiting until the ball reaches the batter's box. They're too anxious to win the game, so they lose it."

We may not always know what others want. When that's the case, why not ask? When asking feels inappropriate, we can probably assume that others want, in today's parlance, to be seen and to be heard. Start by acknowledging those around you, greet them with a smile, and listen to them. When you get to know them, you can better evaluate what they most desire and appreciate. In the meantime, you are laying the foundation for good relationships and great interactions.

# CHAPTER SEVENTEEN

# Share Your Ideas

As we've seen, considering the desires and needs of others goes far in ensuring our success. Another way of directing our attention outward is to consider ways to improve our employer's business. This might be saving money, saving time, or even making employee interactions run more smoothly. Anyone running a business appreciates having a staff member who volunteers his or her ideas for the betterment of the organization. Even if our idea is not adopted, the fact that we are trying to contribute to the business's success will be noted and appreciated by those we work with and for.

Ellis A. Gimbel Jr. was executive head of Gimbel's big New York department store, and vice-president of the Gimbel chain of department stores that extends from coast to coast. He employed between 3,000 and

4,000 people in his New York store alone. His business brought him in daily contact with thousands of people. I watched him at work.

Mr. Gimbel brought out three points that you can use immediately to help you get a job, win recognition in your job, and deal with people more effectively both in business and in your home.

Mr. Gimbel told me, "Most of our employees are salespeople. We don't demand brilliance in our sales staff, and we are not insistent on a college education, but we do want people who can put their heart into their work and make the customers feel that it is a pleasure to serve them."

And how badly such salespeople are needed! Let me tell you what happened to me. One day, I was walking down Fifth Avenue when a necktie in a store window caught my eye. I went into the store to buy it. Several salespeople were idle, but no one greeted me at the door.

I walked halfway down the store until I reached a couple of salesmen lolling on the furniture, talking to one another. I had to stand in front of them before they even looked at me. Then one of them asked in a lifeless manner what I wanted. I told him I wanted a solid blue tie like the one displayed in the window. Did he offer to get it for me? No. He looked toward the back of the store and yelled, "George!"

George was evidently engaged, so with an air of resignation this chap condescended to wait on me himself. He pointed to a case of neckties and said, "See one in there you want?" I found one, and he walked away with it in a bored, listless manner and took so long to get it wrapped that I had to tell him I was in a hurry. Finally, he handed me the package with a dreamy-eyed expression, as if he was thinking of the date he had that night, and he let me walk out of the store without even thanking me for my patronage.

Mind you, that happened in a store on Fifth Avenue—one of the finest shopping streets on earth. It seems incredible that in a big city like New York, where thousands of people are unemployed, it is difficult to get salespeople who will wait on customers in a way that will make them want to return to that store again.

Many young people are unemployed and wondering how they can get a start in life. One of the best ways I know of to get a good flying start in business is by becoming a salesperson. That is the way I started when I left college.

I asked Mr. Gimbel if he thought the field was overcrowded.

"It is overcrowded with incompetents, Mr. Carnegie," he replied. "But it never has been and never will be overcrowded by the right kind of people."

Yes. Business is always looking for salespeople who can go out and get orders—orders that will keep the smoke pouring out of factory chimneys. Good salespeople are in demand in good times, in hard times, and in all times. For example, Harold Sigmund, president of the Afta Solvents Corporation in New York, told me that he advertised in the Sunday papers for salespeople, and he had the big employment agencies send him people who wanted to sell. He even gave good salespeople a drawing account against commission, yet he found it extremely difficult to get intelligent, neat-looking people with personality who would go out and call on customers for eight hours a day, week in and week out, and use common sense and enthusiasm in selling his product.

Here is the first point. You men and women who are wondering how you can get started in business—let me suggest that you try salesmanship. Remember, it takes persistence. It takes personality. It takes self-confidence and hard work. But the rewards are great for those of you who are willing to play the game

This field isn't limited to young men and women only. I was talking last week with Mr. E. H. Little, head of Colgate, and he told me that back in 1917, he had a group of young men and women selling Colgate's soap. Then suddenly World War I came, and many of his salespeople were drafted into the army, so he was forced to go out and hire salespeople who were forty and fifty years old, and he said that those older men and women made one of the best sales forces he ever had.

Mr. Gimbel agreed: "We often find in many of our departments that a mature person has a definite advantage. For example, if a customer is going to buy a fur coat or some furniture or a carpet, they would much prefer to be waited on by a man or woman with experience and judgment. One of the biggest lessons I have learned is that too many young people will ruin a business—and too many old people will ruin it. Every business of any size should have both age and youth."

Here's another point: youth and age must work together for the advancement of both. Youth and age must collaborate. Don't think this applies only in business; it applies in the home too, right in the family. Youth has energy, ideas, and a driving ambition to get ahead, but youth can save itself a million headaches and disappointments if it will sit down and take counsel with age. Older people too profit if they let themselves be stimulated by the open-mindedness and undaunted enthusiasm of youth.

So Mr. Gimbel was looking for salespeople with enthusiasm and enterprise as well as the proper balance of age and youth in his organization. He also said that he looked for people with ideas. "You'll be pleased to know that some of our very best ideas come from people who are in relatively small positions," he said. "For example, we had a porter who tended the incinerator way down in the third basement. He came to us one day and said, 'I wonder if you realize how much stuff you throw away that could be used over again.'

"We asked, 'What do you mean?'

"'Oh, I know they don't look like much—old rusty fixtures and things like that. They're dumped downstairs because they're tarnished and battered up, but isn't there some way they could be repaired? If you put a man down there to watch what goes in that incinerator, you'll save an awful lot of money.'

"We said, 'Fine: that's a good idea. You thought of it, so you're promoted. You take over the job.'"

That porter, by thinking about his work and keeping his eyes open, earned himself a raise in pay and a promotion and saved the firm hundreds of dollars.

Mr. Gimbel gives another example of an employee with ideas. "We had a young woman who was working as a copywriter in the advertising department. She came to us and complained that the shoulder straps on her slip kept falling over her shoulders when she had to hang on to a strap in a crowded subway. She said if it happened to her, it must happen to every woman. So with the help of a manufacturer, we introduced a slip that overcame this difficulty. It was advertised from coast to coast, and women bought it by the thousands."

Here is the third point I want to bring out now: all employers are looking for people who are on the alert to discover new ways and means of improving the business. These people—the people with ideas—are the first to get a raise in pay or a promotion. So why don't you look over your job tomorrow and see if there isn't some way you can save your employer money or time, or contribute to the efficiency of your organization?

When you're on the job, you develop firsthand experience about how your work might be better performed or how your employer might save money. This type of information is invaluable to an employer: sharing your observations in a way that is objective (not self-righteous or self-congratulatory) is bound to be very much appreciated. This is one time where it is good to speak up! You may or may not receive anything concrete for your suggestion, but those around you will be aware that you see the interests of the organization as important. In turn, you further their perception of you as someone they trust and like to have as part of their team. Remember, your idea doesn't have to be completely novel. If you recall a way of saving power for the office that was used at your last job, don't keep it a secret at your new one.

# CHAPTER EIGHTEEN

# The Only Way to Win an Argument Is to Avoid It

**D**id you ever win an argument? For years I tried to win arguments. I was born in Missouri: I had to be shown. In college, I specialized in debating, and I am ashamed to confess that I seriously thought of writing a book on how to win an argument. But I have now come to conclude that ninety-nine times out of a hundred, an argument ends with each person being more firmly convinced than ever that he or she is right. You cannot win an argument, because if you lose it, you lose it, and if you win it, you lose it, because you have triumphed over the other person and made him or her feel small.

"A person convinced against their will is of the same opinion still." So one of the most important rules in dealing with people is this: never tell a person he or she is wrong. Remember that the only way to win an argument is to avoid it.

One man, Archie Danos, argued himself into all kinds of trouble. He was a landlord in New York City and also managed large apartment buildings.

"I was born in Texas," said Mr. Danos, "and when I came east, I hit New York like a cyclone. I expected to flatten out the town. I wasn't taking anything from anyone. I never admitted that a tenant in one of our apartment houses had cause for complaint. I argued and fought with the tenant every time. I won the arguments, all right, but I didn't win business. I wasn't flattening out the town—the town was flattening out me.

"I had one tenant who was always finding fault, always complaining. Finally she refused to pay her rent. So I went around to see her and ask what was wrong.

"'What's wrong!' she said. 'I'll show you! Look at that windowsill! The paint's peeling off! It's a disgrace! No service! No attention! All you think about is collecting your rent!'

"'Sure,' I said, 'the paint's is peeling off. Why shouldn't it? You've been scrubbing it with soap and water. No paint finish in the world will stand that.'

"'But it gets dirty! It has to be scrubbed!'

"'That's not up to us. We're not responsible for the damage tenants do after they move in.'

"'I suppose you're not responsible for heat or hot water either! I never can get any hot water after midnight, and the radiators are ice-cold after eleven!'

"'That's mighty funny. None of the other tenants have complained. You probably turn your radiators down during the day and then forget to turn them up. Of course it gets cold. And there's plenty of hot water all night if you let the tap run long enough. Now what's this complaint about the people upstairs?'

"'Either they go or I go! That woman upstairs— she walks around all night, clicking her heels on the floor! It drives me crazy!'

"'Well, you certainly don't expect me to tell people they can't walk around in their own home.'

"'But I tell you I can't sleep! I'm on the verge of a nervous breakdown!'

"'Now, look here, Mrs. Peterson. There are eighty-six tenants in this building, and we cannot run this building for one tenant; this is an apartment house. You've got to expect some noise. If you want things run just to suit you, why don't you live in a private house? Now let's get down to this matter of rent that's overdue.'

"'Rent! Rent! There you go. I want service. I can't sleep, and you talk about rent! Well, you won't get one cent of rent out of me until you treat me right! Not one red cent! I refuse to pay.'

"'Oh, so you won't pay your rent! Then let me remind you, Mrs. Peterson, that when you moved in here, you signed a lease. If I don't have that rent in two days, I'll take legal proceedings to put you out.'

"I didn't collect that rent," Mr. Danos continued. "But just about that time, I happened to read a book called *How to Win Friends and Influence People*, which made me suspect that something was wrong with me, not my tenants."

Archie came to see me, and I told him that he could starve to death winning arguments in business. People don't want you to prove to them that they're wrong: they want you to listen to them, sympathize with their complaints, and see their point of view.

The next time Archie went to see that tenant, Mrs. Peterson, he used a little sense. He didn't argue. He called on her again and said, "'I don't blame you one bit for being angry. You have had reason to complain.'

"'You bet I have!'

"'Now this is your home, Mrs. Peterson. You're paying hard-earned money to live here, and we want to make it as cheerful and comfortable as possible for you.'

"'It certainly hasn't been cheerful and comfortable up to now!'

"'Now, about that windowsill. We'll paint it over and give it a coat of heavy wax. Then I'm sure it'll stand any amount of washing. Can I send a man up to fix it tomorrow?'

"'Tomorrow? Let me see. Yes. Tomorrow's fine.'

"'I've talked to the people upstairs too. The woman up there is sick, and it's the nurse's footsteps you hear. I asked her if she would mind wearing rubber heels. She didn't realize she was annoying anyone.'

"'Oh, somebody is sick? I'm sorry I complained.'

"'Now are you having any trouble with the hot water?'

"'The hot water? Oh . . . er . . . no, Mr. Danos. As a matter of fact, you were right about that. There's plenty of hot water; I just hadn't been letting it run long enough.'

"'Is there anything else we can do for you?'

"'Why, at the moment, no, Mr. Danos.'

"'If there is, please call me personally. We want you to be not only satisfied but happy about living here.'

"'Why, thank you, Mr. Danos.'"

That was a change. Mr. Danos didn't argue; he saw things from her point of view. He gained her good will. And he didn't even mention the rent. Did he collect it?

"It was in the next morning's mail!" said Mr. Danos. "Mrs. Peterson is still one of our best tenants, and I haven't had a single complaint from her since."

A young man named John Johnstone wrote to us saying that unless he learned how to get along with the people in his office, he feared he would be fired. He was only twenty years old, but unless he changed his ways, he was afraid that he would find himself without friends, without finances, without a job, and without any hope of ever getting another job. Mr. Johnstone was an advertising man, designing ads and making layouts.

Here is an example of what took place in his office. Mr. Johnstone and Mr. Roberts, another layout man, were standing looking out the window.

Mr. Johnstone said, "I tell you, Roberts, old man Wetherby is just a stuffed shirt. He doesn't know as much about running this business as the office boy. It's a miracle to me that we've got any accounts left."

"Oh, I guess we do pretty well," said Mr. Roberts.

"Pretty well, ha! I could take this business and pull it right up out of the mud. What this place needs is pep, new blood, and new customers."

"Say, we'd better get started on these two full-page ads for tomorrow's paper. We better do Thompson's first."

"Thompson's first? You're crazy. Monroe's is the most important."

"But Thompson is running a special campaign."

"So what? We make twice as much money from Monroe's account in the long run."

"Listen, we have two rush jobs," said Mr. Roberts. "We can't stand here arguing."

"I'm not arguing. I'm simply stating facts. Do you know how much money Monroe spends with us in a year?"

"I don't know, and what's more, I don't care. We ought to get started, or we'll be arguing here all night."

"I bet I could handle that Thompson account. I could argue them into doubling their appropriations."

"Hey, take it easy." said Mr. Roberts. "The old man has been standing over there by the water cooler, and I bet he heard everything you said."

"Yeah? Gee!"

Mr. Wetherby, the boss, gave Mr. Johnstone a bawling out about arguing and not minding his own business, and a week later, he fired him.

I asked Mr. Johnstone if he often started arguments during working hours.

"Well, I kept trying not to," he replied. "But gee, when you know you're right and the other fellow's wrong, you have to say something."

"What makes you so certain you're always right?" I asked him.

"Oh, I know," he said. "I read a lot. I've got an encyclopedia at home called the Lincoln Library, and when we had an argument at the office, I proved I was right by the book."

"You mean you actually brought the book to the office?"

"Of course I did."

"Don't you find that makes you a little bit unpopular?" I asked.

"I try to keep still, but I can't. When I hear someone make a statement that I know is wrong, I get so excited, I break out in a cold sweat on the back of my neck."

"Well, well. So you regard yourself as a self-appointed committee of one to correct everyone," I told him. "To tell you the truth, you remind me of myself years ago. Talk about being from Missouri! I was born there. I spent the first twenty years of my life there, and I had to be shown. I argued until I was blue in the face. In fact, I've done just what you did. I've brought down books and proved to people they were absolutely wrong and I was absolutely right. But where did it get me? I won arguments, all right, but I lost friends.

"You know, Mr. Johnstone, Benjamin Franklin was a lot like you when he was a young man. He wrangled and argued. He contradicted everybody who didn't agree with him. One day an old Quaker took him aside and said: 'Look, Ben, you're a smart young man. But do you realize that you give the impression you know it all? Nobody can tell you anything. If anybody disagrees with you, they are absolutely wrong.

You are not going to have many friends or get very far in life until you change your ways.'

"That taught Benjamin Franklin a lesson. He stopped arguing immediately. In fact, he became so adroit and diplomatic that he was later appointed the American ambassador to France, and he says in his autobiography that he owed his success in life largely to the lesson that old Quaker taught him."

"But what would you advise me to do?" Mr. Johnstone asked.

"I would advise you emphatically to stop arguing. Nobody likes to be told their wrong. Here's a safe bit of advice from Benjamin Franklin himself: 'If you fight and wrangle and contradict, you may achieve a victory sometimes, but it will be an empty victory, for you will have lost the other person's goodwill.'

"Remember, no one likes to be told that they are wrong. The next time you hear someone make a statement that isn't true, close your lips tight and refuse to say a word. Not one word. Then, if you stay mad, wait until you get home and write him a letter. Write a scorching letter that will burn up the paper. Then put it away for three days before you mail it. If you do that, you'll probably never mail it. For as time goes on, Mr. Johnstone, you will find that arguments will always cost you the price you have just paid—the loss of your job."

Think back to a time when you got into an argument with someone. How did you feel when the discussion was over? Did you feel happy that you "won" the argument? Did you feel angry or ashamed that you "lost" it? There is no real victor at the close of an argument: both people feel bad.

If you're thinking, "I'm glad when I win an argument, because I've established that I'm right," ask yourself if that is really true. Does it feel good to be self-righteous? Does it feel good to put someone in their place? If it does, how long does that feeling last? Does it feel as though you've created a nice understanding from which to have positive interactions with that person in the future?

The next time you find yourself in a contentious situation, try taking a new approach to the discussion. You'll find that others rarely retain a combative posture when you drop yours. Rather than telling the other person that he or she is wrong, try to see the other person's point. Don't keep repeating your perspective as though it is the only possible truth. Just allow that the other person's understanding is valid. If you cannot say, "You're right" because you are certain that the other person is not right, and you don't want to establish that his or her perspective is true (for example, that you caused a fender bender by negligent driving), that doesn't mean that you must argue. You can instead say, "I don't feel that way, but I understand that you do," or even "Let's agree to disagree about that." This expression may be overused, but it's better to be trite than a bully.

# CHAPTER NINETEEN

# Ensure Good Relationships with Others

A surefire way to ensure good relationships with others is to let them know that we genuinely care about them. One method is to make the effort to remember people's names.

Remember that no other sound on earth is quite so sweet to person's ears as the sound of their own name. Few other compliments you can pay a person are more effective than remembering their name correctly and using it often.

Let me illustrate. A short time age, I attended a dinner dance at a country club. I noticed one young woman there who was extremely popular, and I asked her the secret of her popularity.

"I'll tell you," she said. "It's all very simple. When I am introduced to a young man, I take particular pains to remember his name. I make a point of getting it right, and I address him by his name while we are dancing. When he asks me for another dance, I again use his name. That shows I have been interested enough in him to remember. That is my secret," she confessed.

That young woman was using one of the oldest popularity secrets in the world—a secret that is just as powerful in business as it is in social life. It is a secret you and I can use tomorrow to win friends and influence people.

One man who achieved an outstanding success in business largely because of his ability to remember names was John L. Horgan, and he managed hotels for a number of years. Incredible as it sounds, John L. Horgan could call almost half a million people by name. Scores of newspapers and magazine articles were written about his astonishing memory, and Robert Ripley used him in one of his "Believe It or Not" cartoons.

Mr. Horgan explained how he developed his amazing memory for names: "That's a lesson I learned early in my career. When I first started in business, I worked with a room clerk who had a poor memory. He couldn't even remember the name of a man he had met the same day, but he made a point of greeting each guest by name—and he kept me around to remember names for him. So I decided that one of the best ways for me to get ahead quicker in the hotel business would be to specialize in remembering people's names.

"I believe that 75 percent of whatever success I've had is due to that ability. In fact, being able to remember a man's name proved the turning point in my career. It gave me my first position as manager of an important hotel."

Here's how it happened. It was at the Hotel Statler in Cleveland, Ohio. A distinguished-looking man came through the revolving door, and Mr. Horgan walked over and greeted him.

"Good afternoon, Mr. Nicola," he said; "it certainly is a great pleasure to have you staying with us."

"Oh, er, good afternoon," said Mr. Nicola. "But how did you know my name? I've never been to this hotel before."

"Why, you're Mr. F. F. Nicola of Pittsburgh. I remember you from the Union Club back in 1907."

"That was twelve years ago. That's astonishing. So you have remembered my name for twelve years. Were you a member of the Union Club?"

"I was not. As a matter of fact, I was one of the cashiers."

"And you remembered me after twelve years."

"I knew you almost the second you walked in, Mr. Nicola."

"Well, well, well; and what are you doing here?"

"I'm the associate manager of this hotel."

"The associate manager? What's your name?"

"John L. Horgan."

"Well, shake hands, Mr. Horgan. I'm mighty glad to meet you. I think you're the very man I'm looking for."

"Looking for?"

"Yes, I'm president of the Schenley Hotel in Pittsburgh."

"Yes, I know, Mr. Nicola. As a matter of fact, I started at the Schenley when I was beginning my hotel career. I was the food checker in the kitchen."

"Hmm . . . You started as a food checker. Well, how would you like to go back there as manager?"

"Manager? Of the Schenley?"

"That's right. If you can remember half the names of all the guests at the Schenley the way you remembered my name, then you're the man I want in charge there. I've been in business a good many years, Mr. Horgan, and I have discovered the enormous importance of being able to remember names. Would you like the job?"

"I would be delighted to come to Pittsburgh and be the manager of the Schenley."

Mr. Horgan was a perfect example of the fact that remembering a person's name pays dividends.

"Remembering a person's name actually proved the turning point in my life," said Mr. Horgan. "It made me the youngest manager of an important hotel when I was twenty-six years old. I have managed three major hotels up to now in my career. Here is an astonishing fact: remembering that one man's name secured for me four different offers from five different hotels to act as manager. The moment the Schenley wanted me, three other major hotels began bidding for my services."

Recalling peoples' names is a great way to let you know that you're interested in them. It's good first step in having others want to get to know you better, but where to go from there?

Have you ever faced the problem of how to get and hold a person's interest? We are all confronted with that difficulty almost every day in our business and social contacts. To salesmen it is particularly important.

One man who had an interesting story of how he once handled that problem was James Adamson, president of the Superior Seating Company of New York. At one point, he wanted to get a big order from Mr. George Eastman, of Kodak fame, who at the time was building the Eastman School of Music and Kilburn Hall.

Mr. Adamson went up to Mr. Eastman's office in Rochester, New York, and saw his architect. "He warned me if I took more than five minutes of Mr. Eastman's time, I wouldn't stand a ghost of a show of getting the order," recalled Mr. Adamson.

But when he went into Mr. Eastman's office, Mr. Adamson said, "You know, Mr. Eastman, I am in the interior woodwork business, and I have never seen a more beautiful office in all my life. This wall paneling is English oak, isn't it?"

"A friend who specializes in fine woods selected it for me," said Mr. Eastman. "Look at this grain. See how beautifully figured it is."

Mr. Eastman spent a quarter of an hour walking about the room, pointing out to Mr. Adamson the proportions and the colorings, the hand carving and other effects that he had helped plan and execute in his office. That five-minute interview lengthened into a pleasant two-hour chat.

Mr. Adamson saw a camera in a glass case and he remarked, "That is certainly an old-timer."

"Yes," said Mr. Eastman, "but that's one of my most precious possessions. It is the first camera I ever owned. It fascinated me so that I could think of nothing else. I worked in an office all day and had to conduct my experiments in photography at night. Sometimes I worked and slept in my clothes, without even undressing, for seventy-two hours at a stretch.

"I'll tell you what: why don't you come up to the house with me and have lunch? I want to show you some Japanese chairs I've been painting. Would you like to see what kind of a job I can do painting chairs?"

Mr. Adamson was supposed to have only five minutes of Mr. Eastman's time, and yet they talked for four hours.

"I didn't expect to get this order that same day," said Mr. Eastman, "but I made up some samples, and a few weeks later Mr. Eastman gave me an order for $90,000 worth of seating equipment."

Professor William James of Harvard once said, "The deepest principle of human nature is the craving to be appreciated." Now when James Adamson admired Mr. Eastman's office and his tremendous accomplishments, naturally Mr. Eastman was pleased. Out of that pleasure developed both a social and business friendship.

Benjamin Disraeli was one of the wisest men who ever helped rule the British Empire, and when he was premier of England, Disraeli said, "Talk to a man about himself, and he will listen for hours."

Now am I talking about flattery? Am I talking about saying something nice that you don't really mean so that you can get something out of the other person? No, no! That won't fool anybody. No, I am not talking about flattery, for flattery is selfish and insincere. It won't work.

But I am saying that if we'll forget about ourselves and become unselfishly interested in other people, we'll make friends without even thinking about it, and we will probably increase our income too, because in the last analysis we usually do business with people we like.

So let's make this our how to win rule: let's stop talking about how important we are and start expressing our sincere admiration for the other man's good points. Start tomorrow, and apply this rule during the coming week.


I once received a letter from a young man; it touched me so deeply that I determined to get in touch with him as soon as possible. His name was Edwin McDowd, and he said in his letter that he hadn't a friend in the world except his wife. (It may interest you to know that I received many letters from people who can't seem to hold friends.)

Although Mr. McDowd may have had a number of serious faults, he had some exceptional virtues as well. For example, he permitted me to cross-examine him at length, and he consented to let me analyze his faults in the sincere hope that he could help others with the same problem. It takes courage to do a thing like this—courage very few people possess.

I asked Mr. McDowd what he did when he first met someone.

"I try to make a good impression on them and tell them about myself. I tell them about things I am interested in. I tell them about the interesting experiences I've had. I tell them what I think and what I want to do."

"Don't you realize the impression that makes on the other person?" I replied. "You start talking about yourself. You say 'I, I, I.' You tell people your life's history. In short, you monopolize the conversation."

"I never looked at it that way before, Mr. Carnegie. I was just trying to be interesting."

"Mr. McDowd, the secret of being interesting is very simple. To be interesting, you must be interested in the other person. Do you know who is the greatest winner of friends in the world?"

"No, who?"

"A puppy. Yes, a little puppy knows more about the art of winning friends than all the philosophers and psychologists that ever lived. If you pat him on the head and give him a few words of kindness, he will almost jump out of his skin because he is so glad to see you. You know he doesn't want to get anything out of you. He is not trying to sell you anything. He is not trying to impress you with his importance. The only thing he wants is just the privilege of being with you and loving you. No wonder everybody in the world loves a puppy. It is just the same with human beings. If you are glad to see me and if you are interested in me, I am glad to see you, and I am going to be interested in you. So your first rule for winning is to stop thinking about yourself and start thinking about the other person. Why should people like you if you do not show any interest in them?

"Now, Mr. McDowd, you told me that everyone dislikes you except your wife."

"Mr. Carnegie, I can honestly say that my wife and I have never had a quarrel or a moment's unpleasantness."

"Mr. McDowd, thousands of people who heard that would probably envy you from the bottom of their hearts. You have here a beginning for future happiness that no money on earth can buy, but did you ever stop to figure out why you get along so well with your wife?"

"I love my wife."

"That's just it. You love your wife. You're interested in her. You don't have to try to impress her. And you do all you can to make her happy. She loves you, and she's interested in you. Why not realize that the same principle applies to your relations with other people, too? As a matter of fact, most of your faults are due to self-consciousness and overeagerness.

"You have so much to begin with. You know, you have a pleasant expression. You've got a likable smile.

You're willing to admit your faults, and you're eager to learn. I don't think you'll have any difficulty in holding friends if you'll follow this how to win rule: if you want other people to be interested in you, you must be interested in them. So stop thinking about yourself. Stop talking about yourself. Stop trying to impress other people with your importance. Now try this rule, Mr. McDowd, for if you apply it conscientiously, you will find that people just can't help liking you."

These ideas about conveying our interest in others may seem self-evident, but how often do we forget to put them into practice? How often are we introduced to someone and not even listen to the name of the person we're meeting? In that moment, many of us are thinking about ourselves: "Am I smiling and making eye contact and shaking hands in a way that is purposeful but not overly macho? Is there food stuck in my teeth?" Or we're sizing up the other person: "Wow, great skin! Did I meet her at the last event here? Is this his girlfriend or his friend?" And the name we hear never sinks in.

It can take many attempts to have the practice of remembering someone's name to become a habit. But what an excellent habit to create! Aren't we impressed when someone meets us and then uses our name?

Clearly, the idea of conversing with others about themselves is not generally practiced either. If it were, many of our discussions would be a volley of back and forth "How are yous?" We may want to be entertaining and regale those we meet with our stories, but as a rule, those we meet really want to be heard. We'll find that our conversations are much more rewarding if we draw others out, ask them about their passions, and simply allow them to express themselves. The person with whom we're speaking will have a good memory of the time spent with us, and we will learn things about the person that will help us interact with him or her later. But if we do all the talking, we learn very little about those around us or about how to be sensitive toward and effective with them.

# CHAPTER TWENTY

# Listen: Try to See Things from the Other Person's Point of View

Being a good conversationalist, a good companion, and certainly a good businessperson requires us to listen. This means not just waiting for the appropriate time to reply to someone's comment, but also really hearing what someone is saying. Regardless of who is speaking or the topic, listen carefully to the words chosen by the person with whom you're speaking. You might even try the technique of active listening, in which you rephrase the person's statement and repeat it back to him or her. If not done in a way that seems obvious and overly deliberate, this technique is a great way to engage the person that you're speaking with and let him or her know that you are truly attending to them.

By listening carefully to others and getting them to share their desires with us, we are able to befriend them, obtain their trust, and serve their needs. This is how we develop good relationships.

As Henry Ford said, "If there is any one secret of success, it lies in the ability to get the other person's point of view and see things from their angle as well as your own."

One man who profited from that advice was the smallest dealer in lubricating oil in New York City, a strictly one-man concern. He went into competition against the largest oil companies on earth, yet he beat them and took business away from them.

Of course, I realize that you are not necessarily a salesperson. But when we come right down to it, aren't we all in sales in some form or another? If we are not trying to sell a product, then we are trying to sell our services, our ideas, our enthusiasm, or our personalities. We are selling ourselves to the world, trying to win friends.

So we can all learn a valuable lesson from the way this man solved his problem. His name was Herb Williams, and he ran the Williams Lubricating Company. He was his own salesman, his own bookkeeper, his own stenographer, and his own office boy. He had no one helping him, yet he took business away from companies that were backed by millions.

When he started out, he had pretty hard sledding for the first five years. In fact, he was just about keeping his head above water.

He called for years on the Borden Company, one of the biggest dairy products companies in New York City. They had over 8,000 delivery wagons and trucks, and they bought thousands of pounds of axle grease every month.

"I tried for years to land that order, but I never got to first base," he said. "Nothing was particularly wrong, but the purchasing agent, Mr. Mohr, always told me they were satisfied with the grease they were using.

"I told him a lot about lubricating grease. I told him what kind of axle grease he ought to use; I told him I could save him money if he would give me a trial.

"I know lubricating greases pretty well. I certainly ought to, because I started working in an oil refinery when I was just a kid. I learned the business from the ground up. I showed the buyer that I knew far more about lubricating greases than he did, and I couldn't understand why he wasn't interested. Then one night I happened to listen to your radio program, and I suddenly realized why I was not getting anywhere with him: because I was doing all the talking and showing how much I knew. But this program gave me the idea that I ought to be a good listener and let the other man do a lot of the talking and think in terms of his problems. I thought that over for about a week, and then I went to Borden's again.

"I said, 'I realize that you're busy, Mr. Mohr. But when you get a minute, I'd like to ask your opinion about something.'

"'My opinion? About what?'

"'You've been purchasing lubricants for a number of years. You must know a great deal about the different kinds of lubricating greases.'

"'Listen, Mr. Williams. Two years ago I set out to study every axle grease on the market—every one of them. I took the products of every company that says it can make oil and grease, and I had our chemist analyze all of them, and none of them were what we wanted. So I made up a new grease, and boy, it is a honey.'

"'That's just why I came to you, Mr. Mohr. I thought you might be able to help me.'

"'Help you?'

"'Yes. I know how to make greases, but I don't know the precise needs of each customer. So I've come to ask you just what are the things you want in a perfect axle grease.'

"'Well, we have special problems. Our wagons have to be noiseless, because we drive though the streets at two or three o'clock in the morning while people are asleep. If we make too much noise, somebody will call up and raise Cain. So, as I said, we had to make up our own formula. Take a look at this grease here. This is what we're using now.'

"'I see. It's heavy enough to stick well, and yet it won't run out over the wheels.'

"'That's right. Looks easy, but it took months of hard work to get the right mixture.'

"'Congratulations, Mr. Mohr. But suppose I give you that same identical mixture you are now using, and suppose I could sell it to you cheaper.'

"'You couldn't do that.'

"'Well, maybe I could. You see, I haven't a lot of overhead expenses. No stenographer. No fancy office. No executives. No advertising. If I make a penny, it is all pure profit. Why not let me take a sample of that grease and give you a price? I may save you a lot of money.'

"'All right. Here's a can of it. Take it along, and see what you can do.'"

Mr. Williams not only got the order, but he got an additional order for truck grease that he hadn't even solicited.

"I made $1,200 on that one order alone," he said, "and that is a lot of money for a small fry like me."

Mr. Williams had called on that customer every other month for two years and gotten nowhere. Why?

Because he wasn't thinking about this customer's problems. He was thinking about his own problems. He wasn't thinking about how much he could do for the buyer. He was thinking about how much money he could make by selling the buyer.

A lot of salesmen are like that. For example, a life insurance salesman called on me once. Did he talk about what I wanted? No, he couldn't possibly have done that, because he didn't take the trouble to find out what my specific problems were. He began by telling me that he was in a sales contest; he wanted to win the prize, and he hoped I would help him out by taking some insurance. Then he went on to talk about the fact that his company was safe and reliable.

Now what could he have done? Wouldn't it have been far better if he had begun by saying, "Frankly, Mr. Carnegie, I don't know what your financial picture is. I don't know whether you need any more insurance. You may have too much already. I don't know. But wouldn't it be a good idea for us to sit down together and study your whole financial picture and then see whether or not I could offer any suggestions that would help you face the future securely?" Wouldn't that have been a much better approach?

Neither you nor I want to buy anything. If we did, we would go out and buy it. But everybody is interested in solving his problems. And let me repeat what I said previously: you may not be a salesman, but you can use these principles every day, regardless of whether you are a mother, a teacher, an architect, or a dentist, for all of us are constantly trying to win others to our way of thinking. Nobody wants to feel that they are being sold something or told to do something. All of us much prefer to feel that we are buying of our own accord and acting of our own free will. We like to be consulted about our wishes, our wants, and our thoughts.

For example, let's take the case of a man I know. His name is Eugene Wesson. He lost countless thousands of dollars of commissions before he learned the same lesson Mr. Williams learned.

Mr. Wesson was a salesman for a studio that created designs for manufacturers of cloth. He told me that he called once a week every week for three years on one of the leading buyers of fashion designs in New York. This buyer always looked over Mr. Wesson's sketches, but he never bought.

Finally Mr. Wesson realized that he was in a mental rut and that if he was ever going to get ahead, he would have to devote one evening a week to studying the art of handling people. Presently he was stimulated to try a new approach. So one day he picked up half a dozen of the unfinished sketches that the artists were working on. Then he rushed over to this buyer's office and said, "Look, I have called on you over 150 times, telling you what I thought you ought to buy. Now here are some uncompleted sketches. Won't you please tell me how we can finish them up in such a way that they could be of service to you? You know what you want a thousand times better than I do."

The buyer looked at the sketches and said, "All right, leave them with me for a few days, Wesson, and then come back and see me."

Mr. Wesson returned later in the week, got the buyer's suggestions, took the sketches back to the studio, and had them finished according to the buyer's ideas. The result was that all of them were accepted. And the buyer also ordered a lot of other sketches—all drawn according to his own ideas.

Mr. Wesson called on this buyer once a week for three years without selling him a thing. But as soon as he started to find out what the buyer wanted and talked in terms of his interests and his problems, he made $1,600 in commissions within one year.

So let's make this another of our how to win rules: if you want to do business with a person, find out what their special problems are, and then try to help them solve those problems.

Rather than doing all the talking when we're getting to know someone, it's more fruitful to listen. Ask the person to elaborate on what he or she is telling you. If you're discussing a business opportunity, ask about what is and isn't working best in the business arena. Everyone would like to have his or her problems solved, and you'll be a welcome team member if you offer viable solutions.

Ask yourself, "How often do I spend the time in a conversation thinking about the next thing I'm going to say, rather than listening to the content of what the other person is saying? How often do I interrupt?" Again, what people most want is to be heard. So listen.

# CHAPTER TWENTY-ONE

# Instill Confidence
# in Others

D o you know someone you would like to help and inspire? I am going to demonstrate an almost infallible rule for instilling confidence in other people and stimulating them to achieve results that will seem absolutely impossible.

Let me illustrate what I mean by telling you a story about the famous Connie Mack of the Philadelphia Athletics, one of the greatest managers in the exciting annals of baseball. Back in 1913, during a World Series game against the New York Giants, the Athletics found themselves in a tough spot. It was the eighth inning; the score was 5 to 4 against them; and two men were out.

Harry Davis, captain of the team, coming up to bat, said, "Connie, we must have a real pinch hitter in there. Who'll it be?"

Mack ran his eyes along the bench and spotted a brown-eyed rookie who looked pretty scared. Mack decided to give him a fine reputation to live up to, so he said deliberately, "You know very well there's only one man I would trust in a situation like this," and he nodded toward the brown-eyed rookie.

The rookie heard what Mack said, and those words of appreciation filled him with confidence and determination. So the great Connie Mack was depending on him to win the game, was he? Well, he'd show him; he would win it. A moment later he swung at the ball, made a beautiful hit, and won the game for the Athletics.

That brown-eyed rookie, by the way, was Stuffy McInnis, who lived up to Connie Mack's expectations so well that he later became the starting first baseman for the Philadelphia Athletics and became a valuable member of the Athletics' $100,000 Infield, the most famous infield baseball has ever known.

Now I know that you're thinking, "Oh, that stuff is all right in baseball. But how can I use it to stimulate and improve the people I deal with?"

In order to show you how precisely you can use it, I want to tell you about a man who, by using this same method, performed a miracle in changing a human life. He was Mr. Bryson F. Kalt, secretary of the Kalt Lumber Company in New York City.

At one point, Mr. Kalt became interested in social work. One day a minister came to him and said, "There's a boy in Bellevue Hospital who needs your help. He is only fifteen, but he has tried to kill himself three times. The third time he nearly succeeded, but he may pull through if you can make him want to live."

"At first I didn't know what to do," said Mr. Kalt. "But I got the boy's name and address, and went down to the neighborhood where he lived. I talked to everyone who knew him. He had never had a chance, Mr. Carnegie. His family abused him. He'd never known anything but poverty and rebellion. But what finally gave me hope was the gang of kids he hung around with.

"They were as tough a bunch as you could find on the East Side of New York. But they told me that Danny, the boy in the hospital, was the toughest of the lot. He could lick any of them. That gave me so much hope that I went straight to Bellevue and asked to see the boy."

Before going in to see Danny, Mr. Kalt spoke to the nurse in attendance, who said, "He stands a chance to live if he wants to live. Let's go in and see him."

When they went in, Danny said, "What do you want? I never saw you before."

"I just wanted to get a good look at you, Danny," said Mr. Kalt.

"Me? What for?"

"I wanted to see what a good fighter looks like when he's licked. So you're the toughest fighter on the East Side?"

"Who told you that?"

"Everyone on the block. Red Riley is still nursing the black eye you gave him a week ago."

"Yeah? Boy, did I climb all over him."

"That's what I can't get through my head, Danny."

"What do you mean? I can lick any kid within ten blocks."

"Well, I don't know. I don't see any signs of fight in you now."

"Fighting kids is different from—oh, what's the use; you wouldn't understand."

"You mean fighting kids is different from fighting life?"

"Yeah, I guess so."

"I'd like to prove to you it isn't, and I could prove it to you if you would come with me to the rodeo."

"Rodeo? You mean that circus where there are cowboys and broncos?"

"Yes, that's right; the rodeo's coming to town next week. Of course you wouldn't be strong enough by then."

"I wouldn't, huh? Listen, if I just wanted to . . ."

"Of course, if you wanted to. If you weren't a quitter . . ."

"Who's a quitter? Listen, mister, if I wanted to, I could get up and walk this minute!"

"Oh, you could? Well, if you can get up and walk a week from now, we'll go to that rodeo."

"Honest? Say, this isn't a gag, is it?"

"You bet it's not. I'll be back to see you tomorrow. What kind of ice cream do you like?"

"Chocolate."

"OK. And remember that rodeo. It's a date."

That boy did go to the rodeo with Mr. Kalt, and they went to a soda fountain right after.

"Was that rodeo fun!" said Danny. "Gee, those cowpunchers can take it."

"Sure they can take it. They are tough."

"Boy, I'll say they're tough. Did you see the tall guy in the ten-gallon hat? He was thrown from one bronco, and then he rode a bucking bronco bareback, and then he rode a wild steer! Boy, was he tough!"

"That's what you've got to learn to be, Danny," said Mr. Kalt. "Those broncobusters get tossed around like that every night of the week. But they climb right back on another horse the next night, and finally they get so they can ride the orneriest mustang on the plains."

"Yeah, they never give up, do they?"

"That's what you've got to learn to do with life, Danny. You'll never get anywhere if you keep trying to quit."

"Maybe I was just crazy. But it's different now. I'm not going to quit any more. I'll show you."

"You can start showing me tomorrow morning."

"Tomorrow morning?"

"Yes, I got you a job."

"A job!"

"As an office boy. You can work in the daytime and go to school at night."

Mr. Kalt told me, "I doubt any prizefighter ever tried harder to live up to his reputation as a fighter than Danny did. I was the first person who ever showed any confidence in him, and he was determined not to let me down. From that time on, nothing could lick him. And today, Danny Martin happens to be my best customer."

"Danny Martin" wasn't this boy's real name. The man later became president of one of the biggest corporations in America.

If you want a person to develop a certain trait, then praise them highly when they show the slightest evidence of that trait. For example, if you have a child you want to influence to be neater, then be hearty in your approbation every time they show any evidence of neatness. Praise them for their neatness in front of other people. In other words, make them want to be neat.

The same technique will work with your friends and employees. Give them a fine reputation to live up to, and they will exert every effort to deserve your high opinion. For as the late Samuel Vauclain, president of the Baldwin Locomotive Works, once said, "You can easily lead the average person if you show them that you have sincere respect for their ability along some line."

Now let me give you another illustration. I received a letter from a woman in Stockbridge, Massachusetts, who had been listening to my program and applying my principles to her everyday life. Her name was Margaret French Cresson. She was a sculptor and the daughter of the famous sculptor, Daniel Chester French, who made the statue of Abraham Lincoln in the Lincoln Memorial in Washington, D.C.

Mrs. Cresson had a part-time servant whom she suspected of stealing. Now what did Mrs. Cresson do? Did she accuse the servant? Did she have her arrested? No, she said to her, "Mrs. Smith, I want to talk to you. I want to tell you how greatly I appreciate your work. You keep everything so neat and clean. But lately, well, I've been missing things. Little things, and I feel unhappy about it. Now, I'm not going to ask you any questions, but from now on I am going to place the entire responsibility of this studio in your hands, and I am going to trust you absolutely."

What happened as a result of this treatment? Let me quote from Mrs. Cresson's letter: "The woman said nothing, but the effect was amazing. Not only did I never miss another thing, but also from that day on, she dogged my footsteps. She ran errands for me, mailed my letters, and did a hundred and one little things to show her gratitude."

So if you and I want to develop a desirable characteristic in someone we know, let us remember this how to win rule: give the person you want to change a fine reputation to live up to. Show faith in their ability to do what you want them to do.

I got another letter from a man in Chicago who said he had completely revolutionized his methods of dealing with people. His name was W. G. Wood, and he was in charge of the three New York Central warehouses in Chicago.

In his letter to me, he said that he was not only a great deal happier than before but that his business improved in a way that he would not have believed possible in just a few weeks. That's a pretty strong statement.

"I have 149 people working for me in the New York Central warehouses I operate in Chicago," he said, "and every one of them disliked me. They turned their backs when they saw me coming. They worked like the dickens when I was standing right over them, but the minute I left, they sulked. And for eight years they called me 'Wood the slave driver.'

"My job was to get work out of the men and keep down operating costs, and I didn't much care what the men called me as long as I did my job well and satisfied my superiors."

Did bawling them out when they made mistakes get more efficient work out of Mr. Wood's men?

"Well, take this man Mason, for example," said Mr. Wood. "Every time I raked him over the coals, he was so nervous for a couple of hours afterward that he could hardly keep his hands steady. I was like a lot of bosses: I didn't enjoy being tough with the men, but I just thought I had to be. I honestly believed that the only way you could make men work was to drive them."

Did making men so nervous they could hardly work help him cut down on errors?

"On the contrary," said Mr. Wood. "Errors increased! That meant operating expenses increased too. All of our customers were complaining. The company couldn't understand what was wrong, and I was pretty worried. I listened to this program, and one night you told a story about Charles Schwab."

That was the story of how one day Charles Schwab came across a group of his workmen smoking directly under a sign that said "No Smoking Allowed." Instead of criticizing the men, he chatted with them pleasantly for a few minutes. Then he handed them some cigars and said, "I'd appreciate it if you'd smoke these on the outside."

You'll agree, won't you, that a lot of bosses would have pointed at the "No Smoking" sign and yelled, "What's the matter, can't you read?"

"I had to admit to myself that I'd have hit the ceiling too," said Mr. Wood. "I said to myself, 'That Schwab story sounds all right, but I'd like to try that technique on my crew.'

Mr. Wood tried it out after getting a letter from one of the company's best customers saying that they were making as many as three mistakes a day with his company alone. He threatened to give his business to some other warehouse.

"I had to do something—quick," said Mr. Wood, "so just as an experiment, I decided to change my tactics and give the men a little praise.

"What happened was almost a miracle. Operating costs dropped so rapidly in one week that it took my breath away. My men used to make as many as six costly errors in one day. After I started my new approach, they didn't made one single mistake in three weeks. They used to stall around when they finished a job and just pretend to be busy; after this change, they came straight into my office and asked me what to do next.

"They don't call me 'Wood the slave driver' anymore. They call me Bill and treat me like one of themselves."

Exactly how did Mr. Wood change in his treatment of his men?

"Before," he said, "when the men were doing all right, I just said nothing. Now I go out of my way to tell them what a fine job they're doing. When they used to make mistakes, I'd blow up and raise the roof. Now I simply call their mistakes to their attention. The men correct their own mistakes now. I never have to make the same suggestion twice. And another thing: It used to be if a man came to me with an idea, he wouldn't dare say it was his own idea for fear I'd turn it down and make him feel like a fool. Now I encourage all ideas, whether we can use them or not. The result is that the men are thinking about their work and taking pride in the results."

Mr. Wood also got more credit from superiors. "The warehouses have never operated so efficiently or so economically since they were built, so naturally I'm considered a better supervisor than ever before."

The late John Wanamaker, one of the most successful merchants America ever knew, said that he learned early in life that it was foolish to scold. One day, when Wanamaker was making a tour of his great department store in Philadelphia, he saw a customer waiting at a counter. The salespeople were in a huddle at the far end of the counter, laughing and talking among themselves. Did Wanamaker wade into those salespeople and say, "Why aren't you attending to business? Do I pay you to stand there and talk?" No, without saying a word, he slipped behind the counter, waited on the customer himself, and then handed the purchase to the salespeople to be wrapped as he went on his way. They knew what he meant: they knew they were at fault, and they loved him for his tact and consideration in sparing their feelings.

To be sure, if I am your employee, you can make me work harder by criticizing me and threatening to fire me. I will work harder—until your back is turned. But let us remember that constant blame and condemnation makes a person stupid and bewildered, and in the end destroys their confidence and usefulness. Naturally, they will reward you by hating you and condemning you in return. But if you want to increase a person's usefulness and ability—and this doesn't only apply to employees; it applies to everyone in the world, children included—then treat them as though they could not do wrong. Assume that they are capable and responsible. And remember, if you don't make mistakes once in a while, you're not human. So let us take this for our next how to win rule: to get the best out of a person, praise them when they do good work, and be gentle with them when they are wrong.

Let me now read a quotation from a book: "I've spent the best years of my life giving people the lighter pleasures, helping them have a good time, and all I get is abuse and the existence of a hunted man." Who do you suppose said that?

Al Capone, the Chicago gangster! Al Capone didn't blame himself for anything. He actually regarded himself as a misunderstood and unappreciated public benefactor.

Most gangsters regard themselves that way. Dutch Schultz, before he was shot down in Newark, said he was a public benefactor. He wasn't joking either. He meant it.

I had some correspondence with Warden Lawes of Sing Sing Correctional Facility on this subject. Here's an excerpt from one of his letters: "Few of the criminals in Sing Sing regard themselves as bad men. They are just as human as you and I. So they rationalize; they explain. They can tell you why they had to crack a safe or be quick on the trigger finger. Most of them attempt, by a form of reasoning, fallacious or logical, to justify their antisocial acts even to themselves, consequently stoutly maintaining that they should never have been imprisoned at all."

The point is that if Dutch Schultz, Al Capone, and the desperate men in Sing Sing don't blame themselves for anything, then what about the people you and I will be tempted to criticize tomorrow? I had to blunder through this old world for a third of a century before it even began to dawn upon me that ninety-nine times out of a hundred, no person ever criticizes themselves for anything, no matter how wrong they may be.

Did you ever stop to think of the effect that criticism has? It makes the person who is doing the criticizing feel fine. They unload all their feelings. They tell the other person a thing or two, but what effect does it have on that other person? Naturally, it hurts their sense of importance. It wounds their pride. It makes them want to criticize you in return.

When Abraham Lincoln lay dying, Secretary of War Edwin Stanton pointed to him and said, "There lies the most perfect ruler of men the world has ever seen."

But what methods did Lincoln use? Did he indulge in criticism? Do you know when Lincoln lived on a farm back in Buckhorn Valley, Indiana, he used to have a neighbor by the name of Crawford? Old man Crawford had a big red nose. Lincoln didn't like him. So Lincoln wrote poems ridiculing the man's nose, and he wrote letters criticizing some of the other neighbors. He used to drop these letters and poems casually along the road, where they were sure to be picked up.

Some of those neighbors wouldn't vote for Lincoln when he was running for president thirty years later because of his criticisms as a young man. Even after Lincoln became a practicing lawyer, he wrote a letter to a Springfield newspaper criticizing another attorney. But he did this just once too often. He made one man so indignant that he challenged Lincoln to fight a duel. Lincoln couldn't get out of it and still save his honor. So he met this man on a sandbar in the Mississippi River, prepared to fight to the death.

At the last minute, the quarrel was settled peacefully. That taught Lincoln a lesson. From that time on, he never criticized anybody for anything. During the Civil War, Mrs. Lincoln would sometimes condemn the Southern people. And Lincoln would say, "Don't speak harshly of them, Mother, for they are just what we would be in similar circumstances."

No other man in American history had more reason to criticize than Abe Lincoln did. Let me give you just one example. Immediately after the defeat of Robert E. Lee at the battle of Gettysburg, Lincoln saw an excellent chance to win a crushing victory, so he told General George Meade to attack Lee at once. But Meade failed to obey Lincoln's orders. As a result, Lee escaped, and Lincoln immediately sat down and wrote a sharp letter criticizing Meade for not obeying orders. But Lincoln never sent that letter. It was found among his papers after his death. I imagine after writing that letter of criticism, Lincoln looked out of the White House window and said, "What's the use of sending this? It won't help Meade defeat Lee. That's water under the bridge now. It's only going to make Meade criticize and condemn me and justify himself." Lincoln at last had learned the utter futility of criticism and condemnation.

So the next time you or I are tempted to criticize somebody, let's pull a five-dollar bill out of our pocket, look at Lincoln's picture, and ask, "I wonder what Lincoln would do if he were in my place?"

Do you know somebody you would like to criticize and change? Well, I have just one suggestion to make. I think it's rather important too. Remember there are times when certain criticism of others is necessary. Nobody denies that. But as Jesus said twenty centuries ago, and Confucius said 500 years before Jesus was born, "Let's perfect ourselves first." Yes, we must remember to perfect ourselves first. Let's try to figure out why they do what they do. That's a lot more profitable and intriguing than hasty criticism, and it breeds sympathy, tolerance, and kindness.

People change themselves. We can inspire them and encourage them, but we cannot change them.

It should be apparent from the above that criticizing someone will not get us the behavior that we seek. We can see this truth in own our experiences, and it is very applicable to our own lives.

Think first about a time when you were criticized. Did you want to do better the next time? If so, did you want to do better to avoid being criticized again? Was your pride wounded? Did you feel good about yourself? How did you feel about the person who criticized you? Then think about a time when someone praised you. Did you want to continue in the praiseworthy behavior? How did you feel about yourself? How did you feel about the person who praised you?

These simple questions bring home for us the wisdom of maintaining positive interactions. Indeed several of my golden rules for success speak to lifting others up rather than putting them down: Praise the slightest improvement and praise every improvement. Be hearty in your approbation and lavish in your praise. Give the other person a fine reputation to live up to.

Make it your habit to look for, and comment on, the positive behaviors of everyone around you. It will make them happy to know you or work with you, and they in turn will want to make your experience of them always a good one.

CPSIA information can be obtained
at www.ICGtesting.com
Printed in the USA
JSHW050228250522
26133JS00002B/2

9 781722 506094